KU-532-555

PARTNERSHIPS I.
HEALTH PROMOTION:
COLLABORATION BETWEEN
THE STATUTORY AND
VOLUNTARY SECTORS

Leeds Metropolitan University

17 0060609 8

PARTNERSHIPS IN HEALTH PROMOTION: COLLABORATION BETWEEN THE STATUTORY AND VOLUNTARY SECTORS

Written for the Health Education Authority and the National Council for Voluntary Organisations by
JENNY FIELDGRASS

LEEDS POLYTECHNIC

1700606098

TD ✓

3002201   20.10.92

14.1.93

614.44 FIE

First published 1992

Published by the Health Education Authority
Hamilton House
Mabledon Place
London WC1H 9TX

© Health Education Authority 1992

All rights reserved. No part of this publication may
be reproduced, stored in a retrieval system or
transmitted in any form or by any means, electronic,
mechanical, photocopying, recording or otherwise
without the prior permission of the
publishers or a licence permitting restricted
copying issued by the Copyright Licensing Agency Ltd,
33–34 Alfred Place, London WC1E 7DP

ISBN 1 85448 295 5 ✓

Typeset by DP Photosetting, Aylesbury, Bucks
Printed in Great Britain
by Scotprint Ltd., Musselburgh

CONTENTS

FOREWORD

Everyone has a part to play in promoting a healthier society – one in which individuals and communities are encouraged to make informed choices and to achieve their potential.

Health promotion crosses many boundaries and may encompass curative and support health services, social, environmental, economic and fiscal policies; it therefore needs flexibility and co-ordination if effective solutions are to be delivered.

Voluntary organisations also cross many boundaries, and we believe that there is a major role for them to partner health professionals in their work in health promotion, and help provide that flexibility and sensitivity to need.

The National Strategy for Health highlights the need for collaboration at a local level to develop effective local health strategies. Now that collaboration and co-operation are firmly on the National Health agenda, it is timely to get a view of existing successful partnerships between the statutory and voluntary sectors and so gain an understanding of the nature of their success.

We hope this report will provoke new thought and many new partnerships. It could not have been possible without the tremendous amount of support, help, comment and input from the ad hoc group, the Project Advisory Group, many different parts of the National Health Service and the voluntary sector. To all those who have contributed and helped – a very big 'thank you'.

Kay Young
Chair, Project Advisory Group

The following initials appear throughout the report:

NCVO National Council for Voluntary Organisations
HEA   Health Education Authority
HFA   Health for All 2000
RHA   Regional Health Authority
DHA   District Health Authority
HPU   Health promotion/health education unit
FHSA Family Health Service Authority (replaces the old Family Practitioner Committee)
CHC   Community Health Council
CVS   Council for Voluntary Service
WHO   World Health Organisation
NCHR National Community Health Resource
NAHAT National Association of Health Authorities and Trusts

1 INTRODUCTION

Preparation of this report was carried out between mid-April and mid-October 1990, and provides – for readers in both the voluntary and the statutory sectors – a snapshot of the sort of health promotion partnerships that exist between the NHS and voluntary organisations. The report also notes the existence and potential for further involvement of other partners, such as local authorities and commercial organisations.

Because of the limited timescale, the report covers England only and singles out a number of partnerships as examples of 'good practice'. Detailed accounts of 15 of these partnerships are included as Appendix 2. The examples selected reflect the different types of partnership that are taking place: there are examples with a national remit, as well as those which are locally or community-based. It is hoped that this reflects the tremendous variety and ingenuity of projects being carried out today.

For the purposes of this report, 'voluntary' means both large, non-governmental organisations, as well as small, community-based ones. 'Voluntary organisations' are defined here as 'self-governing bodies of people who have joined together voluntarily to take action for the benefit of the community and have been established other than for financial gain'.

'Statutory' means all parts of the NHS, from health promotion officers; members of the primary health care team, such as GPs, health visitors, community nurses; Regional and District Health Authorities; the Department of Health, and special health authorities such as the Health Education Authority.

Also included are other possible partners within the statutory sector, such as other government departments and local authorities, and the corporate sector.

Why is NCVO interested in health promotion?

The National Council for Voluntary Organisations (NCVO) is the main representative organisation for voluntary bodies in England. It is the national voice for voluntary organisations. Its aims are:

- to promote the common interests of voluntary organisations, particularly among policy makers at government level
- to provide, and encourage others to provide, a range of resources that will increase the effectiveness of voluntary organisations
- to extend the scope of the voluntary sector and to identify new areas for action.

It has a commitment to partnership and a continuing interest in all issues affecting voluntary organisations. It maintains a watching brief on these, commenting on emerging government policy and suggesting opportunities for voluntary organisations to influence developments in relevant areas including health care.

NCVO has promoted voluntary interests in the Primary Health Care White Paper,[1] and has provided a response from the voluntary sector to the Health Education Authority's Strategic Plan.[2]

Many of NCVO's member organisations are interested and involved in health promotion in its widest sense – some directly, because they are involved in specific health issues, and some indirectly, through their commitment to environmental or community-based projects.

NCVO's Bedford Square Press has published a number of information directories and other books in the health field, notably *The Health Directory*.

How this report came about

NCVO's interest in the potential for partnership between the voluntary sector and the Health Service was given a focus in 1987, with the publication – jointly with the National Association of Health Authorities – of *Partnerships for Health*.[3] That report discussed the ways in which the voluntary sector was working alongside the NHS at that time, and provided guidelines on a framework for the further development of such partnerships. The perspective of *Partnerships for Health* was incorporated into comments NCVO has since made on specific health legislation – including the NHS White Paper, *Working for Patients*[4] and the National Health Service and Community Care Bill.[5]

Since 1987, NCVO has become increasingly aware of the growing numbers of voluntary bodies that are actively involved in health promotion. This involvement has been evident in all sorts of ways: from the more traditional forms of volunteering, such as driving minibuses, manning information desks or providing advice, to a newer 'model': those that are keen to campaign on health and are even keener to keep themselves at arm's length from the NHS.

> 'People who are active in voluntary agencies:
> 1. Believe they "own" their organisations.
> 2. They also believe they own the issues their organisations are seeking to tackle.
> 3. They also want to "change the world", which is often why they are there.'*

There are also more and more people who have taken a pragmatic approach – actively bringing about change – and the implementation of new ideas – by developing links and joint ways of planning and working with parts of the NHS. This is echoed by the many parts of the NHS that are now becoming more proactive and themselves seeking partnership with both voluntary bodies and, more directly, with the community.

* Unattributed quotation from questionnaire.

Discussions held between NCVO and the Field Development Division of the Health Education Authority late in 1989 highlighted the opportunity for NCVO to carry out an investigation to provide a picture of the extent to which the voluntary sector was becoming actively involved in health promotion; to look at the strengths, weaknesses, opportunities and threats that the partnerships were facing.

Finally, the report aims to draw out some conclusions from the successful collaborations – and to make suggestions on how further partnerships could be developed.

Other factors, it is felt, make this report timely. First, the role of the voluntary sector in today's society. In the words of a working party set up by NCVO:

> Voluntary organisations matter. They matter to those who benefit from the services they provide; to those who give money and time to them; and to the staff who work for them. The quality, scale and diversity of the activities of voluntary organisations mean that, taken together, voluntary organisations matter a great deal to the country. They are also important in economic terms. The most recent available figure for the estimated total income of the voluntary sector, including government grants and receipts from fees and charges, is £15 billion (based on an estimate of £12.65 billion in 1985). This amount is three times the income of the agricultural sector of the [UK] economy . . .[6]

Working in partnership with the voluntary sector is very much on the agenda. Indeed John Patten, Minister for Home Affairs, stated in August 1990:

> We should recognise that the boundaries of voluntary, government and business activities shift all the time. There are no pieces of absolutely inviolable territory for each . . . The government's policy towards the voluntary sector is reasonably clear: try to work in partnership, resisting temptations to take over or bureaucratise . . . support financially . . . listen and consult; borrow some ideas from the voluntary sector innovators; ask the voluntary sector to try out other new ideas; try to keep the relationship fresh and developing . . .[7]

Secondly, the government is moving towards the setting of targets for health care areas. This move, announced in mid-October 1990, will open discussions on providing targets for areas of health such as diabetes, heart disease, cancer and asthma. 'It will provide a way of measuring success and evaluating what we are getting for our investment in the NHS', said Kenneth Clarke, then Secretary of State for Health, launching the initiative.[8] Setting of targets will involve the NHS and the health professionals – and the voluntary sector too will want to have a role at the planning stage.

Thirdly, an increasing interest is being shown by many parts of NHS in the philosophy of 'Health for All'. Health for All (covered in more detail in Chapter 2) is based on the concept of different sectors working together, particularly collaboration with non-statutory partners. Commitment to the Health for All philosophy is one of the criteria used to select partnerships for inclusion in this report.

Finally, the changing shape of the NHS will mean increasing demands for flexibility, entrepreneurialism, and new ways of working. It will also bring a number of opportunities for the voluntary sector, including the possibility of voluntary organisations having a real role to play (should they decide to accept it) as 'providers' of health promotion back into the NHS.

AIMS

The aims of the project were:

- to bring together an advisory group of people with knowledge of collaboration between statutory and voluntary organisations in the field of health promotion, and thus create a network of expertise. A smaller sub-group, the 'ad hoc group', was also convened to take a greater involvement in the management of the project and to make key decisions, such as the selection of projects to be visited. (A list of those who attended at least one of the three meetings is included in Appendix 1.)
- to identify partnerships in health promotion taking place in England, where a voluntary organisation is collaborating with part of the NHS
- to collect examples of good practice in collaboration
- to explore the potential for enhancing existing partnerships, and for creating new ones
- to make recommendations about ways in which such partnerships could be further assisted
- to publish a report endorsed jointly by NCVO and the HEA.

METHODOLOGY

First stage - May 1990

It was recognised that given the timescale of six months to prepare and write the report, it was unlikely that a note of every single partnership in health promotion would be obtained. An initial trawl was carried out to compile a list of known partnerships. There is no one central database containing this information, so separate requests for help (accompanied by questionnaires) were sent to:

- organisations represented on the Project Advisory Group
- appropriate member organisations of NCVO (286 in total)
- Health promotion units and local authority Environmental Health Officers, through HEA's *Liaison News* (now called *HEAdlines*)
- thirty 'Healthy Cities' co-ordinators
- community organisations listed on the National Community Health Resource (NCHR) database
- all Community Relations Officers in England
- organisations known by NCHR Women's Health Network
- appropriate organisations included in the *Health Directory* published by Bedford Square Press
- members of the London Advice Services Alliance
- NCVO's rural members – contacted through NCVO's rural unit
- National Association of Volunteer Bureaux
- a comprehensive list of voluntary youth groups.

In addition, lists of projects that involved a voluntary/community perspective were obtained from:

- the National AIDS Trust
- the Look After Your Heart (LAYH) programme at the HEA
- the AIDS programme team at the HEA
- the Women's Health co-ordinators at the HEA
- the Association of Community Health Councils of England and Wales
- the National Self-help Support Centre.

The questionnaire

An example of the questionnaire is included at Appendix 5. The questionnaire was designed to produce information on the objectives of the partnership, its sphere of interest, the partners involved and what each provided, and to invite a brief comment on the positive and negative aspects that the partnership had encountered. Unattributed quotations from the completed questionnaires have been included throughout this report (distinguished by italics with a light tint behind them). In all, around 1000 questionnaires were sent out.

Second stage - June/July 1990

The ad hoc group assessed each returned questionnaire and arrived at a short-list of projects many of which were visited by the project worker between July and September 1990, in some cases more than once. Projects were selected on the basis that the project was well-established, appeared to be an example of good practice, and included a measurement for evaluation. Wherever possible, the project worker spoke to both the voluntary and the statutory partner. Projects covered in detail have been invited to check and amend the details included in this report.

The case studies - how were they selected?

The case studies in Appendix 2 were chosen as examples of innovative partnerships demonstrating what the group believed to be good practice. They also provide a good cross-section of activities, and highlight the different types of partnerships that can exist both on national, regional, district and local level. The examples

- represent partnerships where voluntary and statutory partners are working closely alongside or together, rather than a situation where the statutory sector was simply funding the voluntary partner
- have aims and objectives which echo the philosophy of Health for All 2000.
- show high quality, practical benefits being provided
- are concerned with equality of opportunity and access for disadvantaged sectors of the community
- use some method of monitoring both the quality and cost-effectiveness of the work.

Other considerations in selecting the projects to visit were:

- the areas of health promotion covered (projects have been chosen as examples of different HEA programme areas, and different 'setting' areas)
- that all projects were in England – Wales and Scotland were specifically excluded
- all the projects had been established for at least one year.

NOTES AND
REFERENCES

1 *Promoting Better Health: the Government's Programme for Improving Primary Health Care*, Cm 249. HMSO, 1987.
2 *Health Education Authority: Strategic Plan 1990–95*. HEA, 1990.
3 *Partnerships for Health*. NCVO/National Association of Health Authorities, 1987.
4 *Working for Patients*, Cm 555. HMSO, 1989.
5 National Health Service and Community Care Bill 1989/90, subsequently becoming the National Health Service and Community Care Act 1990.
6 *Effectiveness and the Voluntary Sector*, Report of a Working Party established by NCVO. NCVO, 1990.
7 John Patten, Minister for Home Affairs, reported in the *Guardian*, 1 August 1990.
8 Department of Health press release 90/487, 9 October 1990.

2 HEALTH PROMOTION – ITS CONTRIBUTION TO HEALTH CARE

Health promotion is the subject of many learned papers and much discussion among health professionals.

WHO (in a discussion document on the concept and principles of health promotion) defines health promotion as 'a unifying concept for those who recognise the need for change in the ways and conditions of living, in order to promote health'.[1]

Health promotion is based on the fundamental and inextricable link between people and their environment. If basic requirements for health are income, shelter and food, then any improvement in health requires not only a secure foundation in these basics but also: information and lifeskills; a supportive environment; providing the opportunity for making healthy choices among goods, services and facilities; and conditions in the economic, physical and social/cultural environment (the 'total environment') which embraces health.

WHO defines five areas as reflecting health promotion:

- creation of a healthy public policy
- creating a social environment conducive to health
- providing knowledge and motivation for health behaviour
- promoting positive health behaviour
- reducing damaging health behaviour.

Health promotion represents the concept of a collective effort by all parts of the population to attain health, aiming 'to enable people to increase control over the determinants of their own health'. It encompasses everything from curative medicine and all facets of the health services, to social, economic and fiscal policy and social services.

Key factors in health promotion are:

- involving the population and developing opportunities for public participation
  (In essence, the 'sharing' of responsibility – an acknowledgement that health is for everyone to do something about collectively and individually – and not just the preoccupation of the statutory sector.)
- taking action on factors that contribute to good health – ensuring that the environment is conducive to health, which may mean lobbying for changes in health policy that will make it easier for people to follow healthier lives (e.g. changes in the regulations on advertising of tobacco)
- increasing knowledge and disseminating information about health
- strengthening social networks and social supports

- supporting the principle of self-help and self-care movements, to allow people to form their own directions for managing the health of their own community
- developing co-operation between different groups.

Health promotion can cover a wide area, going far beyond the remit of local statutory authorities and the Department of Health. The National Health Service therefore ends up concentrating its finite resources in areas where it can be expected to achieve greatest impact – for example, in prevention of coronary heart disease, anti-smoking initiatives and direct intervention in areas like vaccination and immunisation, and health screening.

The HEA's Strategic Plan for 1990–95 acknowledges the importance of health promotion:

> Any strategy to improve the nation's health needs to be comprehensive, incorporating measures such as taxation, legislation, economic development and environmental protection. The role of the government in these measures is vital. But they need to be complemented by other public health measures including health education which, undertaken properly, can make a major contribution to the prevention of disease and the enjoyment of a healthy life.[2]

> 'We started our laryngectomy group in 1986. I first asked the head speech therapist to help because back-up was non-existent. She replied "I prefer stroke victims." A local voluntary group gave me help, and it was their idea to start a newsletter. I moved to the local health information centre when I had problems with the speech therapist - two years later she wanted to take control of a thriving club so she looked good in front of consultants. I refused to allow it and the health information officer came to my rescue - she gave me a room in the information centre, she had my newsletter published and sent to every "lary". I owe her a great deal for helping us.' (letter from secretary of local laryngectomy club)

WHAT IS HEALTH EDUCATION AND HOW DOES IT RELATE TO HEALTH PROMOTION?

Health education has always had, and will continue to have, a pivotal role in all health promotion activities.

In recent years, the thrust of health education has shifted, and become much more directly linked with health promotion. As a WHO committee said in 1983:

> In the early years of health education, relatively few efforts were made to understand people's traditional health beliefs and practices, and to consider these practices in developing health strategies. While some attempts were made to learn about what the communities themselves regarded as their health needs and priorities, these were not systematic. It was assumed, rather, that only health professionals were in a position to assess these needs and priorities... The assumption underlying health education activities was that people would enjoy

better health if they would act in a manner recommended by health workers. Hence, the emphasis was on the transmission of correct health information to the general public.[3]

Current trends in health education

The Health Education Authority is the key provider of health education in this country. It believes that for health education to be effective, it must be based on a thorough understanding of the public's needs, and be undertaken in partnership with others. Like everyone in the real world, it has to work with finite resources, and has elected to concentrate its efforts on a series of programme areas which it sees as priorities for promoting a healthy life, and reducing premature death and disability. Further details about the role and programme areas of the HEA are given on pp. 18–20.

Another body, the Society of Health Education and Health Promotion Officers, stresses that to meet the challenges of today's society, health education is now much more than the 'giving of information':

Health education represents an enormous challenge to everyone in society, and is a massive and ongoing task. Like any educational process, it is concerned with the developing of an enhanced self-image and self-empowerment of individuals and groups. Health education is also concerned to develop skills in areas such as assertiveness and value clarification, and with raising critical awareness in order that individuals, groups, communities and managers can make high-quality decisions about health issues. Health education not only focuses on individual behaviour, attitudes, etc. which must influence health, but also on influencing planners and policy makers.[4]

Areas of health education which the Society of Health Education and Health Promotion Officers considers to be priorities include:

- enhancing the role of all health care and service providers with regard to health education
- the ongoing task of providing high-quality health information
- the developing area of providing patient education and information services
- the support of community-based health promotion initiatives.

'The major obstacle is to overcome any misgivings about the motives of each other and to work together for the good health of local people'. (health promotion unit involved in partnerships with local voluntary organisations)

'HEALTH FOR ALL'

'Health for All' is a pledge to good health. In 1977 the World Health Authority, the World Health Organisation's governing body of 166 member states, resolved that by the end of this century people everywhere should have access to health services that enabled them to lead socially and economically productive lives. This strategy is known as 'Health for All 2000'.

The European region of WHO stressed its commitment to the world-wide strategy by devising a list of 38 targets to be achieved by the year 2000 (a summarised list is given at Appendix 4). How many of these targets really *will* be achieved by the year 2000 is open to debate – many may seem purely idealistic. However, what is just as important are the three key planks which underpin the Health for All philosophy:

- *Reducing inequalities of health*
  the aim to reduce inequalities in health care means ensuring that all members of a multiracial community have direct access to the services and facilities provided by the NHS. This is particularly needed in the case of minority ethnic groups, who have often in the past been alienated and ill-served by traditional health education material. Health for All encourages the involvement of minority groups in producing and disseminating their own health promotion material, in a shape and form that they see as being appropriate to their own community.

> *'Many health professionals still see community organisations as ill-informed and interfering. Community development is an approach not well understood or appreciated.'* (vice-chair of health project management committee, London)

- *Working with the community*
  According to the Health for All philosophy, involving a community or communities is an essential component of health promotion programmes.[5]
  Community participation of any kind is better than no community participation at all. National Community Health Resource (in a 1989 paper) divides community involvement into the following levels:
  Community participation. A process starting from the premise of equality and collective action. It involves empowering people to identify and articulate their needs; enabling them to share their knowledge, skills and experience; facilitating collective action through the process of self-education and self-help.
  Community involvement. The process by which partnership is established between government and local communities in the planning and implementation of health activities.
  Finally – and the ultimate aim – is
  Community health development, which
  1. takes a whole person (holistic) approach
  2. is something done *with* people, not *to* them
  3. is where people are encouraged to define their own needs rather than receive a professionally prescribed list of priorities
  4. is where the emphasis is put on issues common to many members of the community, rather than concentrating on individual problems in isolation
  5. seeks to involve greater participation by the community in their own health and health care delivery.[6]
- *Different sectors working together*
  This involves getting different groups and sectors with very different cultures to work together. It can often be extremely difficult to integrate two

structures that seem similar: as an example, health authorities and local authorities may seem similar to the outsider, but operate very differently, with different management systems, and often covering different territories. There are many natural geographical problems involved for a health authority trying to work with a local authority whose boundaries are not coterminous.

There can be other problems, as were noted at a workshop at NCHR's 1989 conference:

> Professional ambition and competition, territoriality and protectionism are major barriers to bringing agencies together. Information is often seen as a major source of power and so is only shared reluctantly. Different terminology and the use of jargon can also make working together more difficult . . . Political tensions between local authorities and health authorities frequently lead to poor communication and co-operation.[6]

Health for All in practice

So how many people *are* actually putting the high ideals of Health for All into practice? Two surveys give some indication:

First, in May 1990 Alan Beattie of the Centre for Health Research in Lancaster, compiled a picture of the degree to which Health for All was a driving factor in the first round of annual reports on public health, which the Department of Health now requires District Health Authorities to publish.

He found that the inclusion of Health for All varied widely, throughout the 72 DHA reports and 3 RHA reports surveyed. At one end – in a minority of reports – Health for All, was 'either the theme that ran through the whole report, or was a point of reference that was given special attention throughout'. In a few instances, there were examples where HFA targets were used to structure the whole report. Then, in the middle, there were another 20 reports which contained a discrete section on Health for All. In a further 12 reports, Health for All did appear, but only as a restatement of the WHO targets, with no evidence of local application . . . 'The rest of the sample (amounting to almost a half) is revealing in a different way. In these there is no mention whatever of HFA at any point in the report'.[7]

The second survey was carried out in November 1989, by the Institute of Health Service Management, which surveyed all Regional and District Health Authorities on their attitudes towards Health for All. Ninety-seven of the responding 119 health authorities or health boards (81.5 per cent) and 6 out of the 8 responding regional health authorities (75 per cent) had 'made efforts to raise awareness of the HFA philosophy and targets among HA managers, professionals and other staff'. The means of raising awareness included conferences and seminars, discussion papers to staff, covering the subject in staff newspapers, writing HFA into job descriptions, as well as references to HFA in the authorities' public health report. Of responding health authorities and health boards 85.7 per cent claim to have established partnerships with other agencies in working towards HFA. Seven out of the 8 responding RHAs had established partnerships with other agencies (87.5 per cent). Local authorities were most popular as partners (73.5 per cent), followed by voluntary organisations (45.1 per cent).[8]

NOTES AND
REFERENCES

1 WHO. *Health Promotion: Concepts and Principles in Action: a Policy Framework*. WHO Regional Office for Europe, Copenhagen, 1986.

2 *Health Education Authority: Strategic Plan 1990–95*. HEA, 1990.

3 *New Approaches to Health Education in Primary Health Care*, report of WHO Committee. World Health Organisation, Geneva, 1983.

4 J. French, Secretary of the Society of Health Education and Health Promotion Officers, personal communication, October 1990.

5 For a full list of targets and discussion, see *Targets for Health for All: Targets in Support of the European Regional Strategy for Health for All* (WHO Regional Office for Europe, Copenhagen, 1985).

6 Jane Lethbridge, 'Intersectoral working: ideas from conference theme groups', National Community Health Resource, 1989.

7 *HFA 2000 News*, Faculty of Community Medicine of Royal College of Physicians, May 1990.

8 'Health for All Questionnaire – Revised Evaluation', Institute of Health Service Management, 1990.

3 *WHY FORM A PARTNERSHIP TO PROVIDE HEALTH PROMOTION?*

> *'Close collaboration [has meant that] . . . we have become more supportive to each other in other activities as well.'* (health project, London)

WHAT ARE THE ADVANTAGES OF PARTNERSHIP?

In health promotion, where flexibility and novel approaches are a driving need, and no one agency has a monopoly on providing an answer, we believe that partnership represents an ideal way of working.

Perhaps the easiest way to describe the greatest benefit of partnership is by using the word 'additionality'. This is the concept of 'better together than apart' – the fact that partnerships have the potential to bring together strengths and weaknesses in the hope of making something that far exceeds the sum of the parts.

Partnerships can be dynamic, exciting and different. Learning from each other – and giving to each other – produces new and diverse structures that can grow and develop.

Partnerships do not have a single vision. They have experiences of many sectors and of people outside the mainstream, and will be able to ensure that equity and access are prime considerations at the outset.

Given the emphasis on value for money, partnerships are also a *cost-effective* method of providing health promotion: a small injection of professional skills can reach a long way when it is combined with a network that is close to the community. Likewise, a shot of advice from a community perspective can help shape a professional message into something that becomes ten times more powerful and accurately targeted.

WHAT DOES THE VOLUNTARY SECTOR HAVE TO OFFER?

Given that everyone has a part to play in health promotion, voluntary organisations offer a natural partner for any of the other statutory 'players' who deliver health promotion.

Differences of culture - do they matter?

> *'It has been an uphill battle to gain [their] acceptance as they were anxious about the accountability of volunteers. This has been overcome by their decision to appoint and control a co-ordinator'.* (volunteer bureau servicing a partnership of voluntary group and DHA hospital members)

It is evident from the numbers of partnerships that already exist that voluntary and statutory sector cultures – although often very different – can work together in harmony. Understanding and acceptance is always the key, and this means that both sides will have to go beyond the stereotypical criticisms that each levels against the other: health professionals have sometimes been reluctant to work with the voluntary sector, seeing it as 'unprofessional', 'chaotic', and 'enthusiastically amateur'. Its reliance on volunteers means that people have seen it as 'unaccountable'.

But parts of today's voluntary sector have honed and sharpened their activities. There is more expectation placed on the voluntary sector today, and there are more voluntary organisations than ever before. Some voluntary organisations (even quite small ones) have had to develop 'streetwise' skills for their own survival, such as developing political lobbying to increase support and funding, and running a high-profile campaign through the media.

Using volunteers

> 'There were some doubts amongst the health care professionals as to the reliability of the advice which might be given by people with [this particular illness]. However, these professionals have been reassured by the success of the scheme and the ability of the volunteers to deal with all kinds of problems.' (illness-specific telephone information line)

Volunteers should always be used to improve the quality of service, rather than as a substitute for paid staff. For considerations on the question of using volunteers – and how they should interact with paid staff – see guidelines from the Volunteer Centre in Berkhamsted entitled *Relationships between Volunteers and Paid Non-professional Workers*.[1]

Voluntary organisations and volunteers are quite separate things. Voluntary organisations may well have voluntary management committees, but are usually professionally-run organisations often with quite substantial budgets.

While it is still a sector that 'has room for the enthusiast, and, on occasion, the eccentric',[2] voluntary organisations are having to pay higher salaries to compete with industry and to attract high calibre staff. Consequently, the sector can (and sometimes does) attract the most flexible, entrepreneurial and committed of individuals, who see the 'not for profit' sector as offering a worthwhile (and financially rewarding) life-long career path. Added to this are the growing numbers of secondments from corporate bodies, and entrants at 'career-change' points, such as early retirement.

Sometimes, voluntary organisations may use volunteers in the delivery of services, but often (particularly in the health field), voluntary organisations are increasingly employing highly-qualified medical or other health professional staff as part of their team.

Volunteers have changed, too. While many (if not all) volunteers still have as their prime motive for volunteering the enormous personal satisfaction they get from helping others, members of today's voluntary organisations do not always fit the traditional model.

And, like others working within the statutory and health services, voluntary organisations are dedicated to working with and for the disadvantaged, who have traditionally found it difficult to make their voices heard – the groups that are a key target of the WHO policies.

The voluntary sector is rich and diverse and includes reaching out to minority ethnic groups who might otherwise not be heard. The sector also contains many minority ethnic voluntary organisations, who are able to serve the interests of their own client groups.

It would be easy to paint a glowing picture of the voluntary sector, as being highly professional and highly motivated. But we have to acknowledge that there are many different organisational cultures within it, and many organisations which have not yet grasped the realities that to compete for funding and to survive in a financially-recessive climate, they will have to operate in a businesslike and professionally-managed way.

But cultural exchange is a 'two-way street'. It is only fair to say that the voluntary sector does not always see the statutory services through 'rose-tinted spectacles'. 'Rigidly bureaucratic', 'condescending and patronising', 'a blank wall full of red tape', and 'keen to only disseminate leaflets and literature', are some of the ways that voluntary organisations describe health service providers.

In summary, voluntary organisations can provide:

- flexibility – of structure and approach
- a sense of vision – because they are less dependent on satisfying either line-management needs or a 'bottom line' on the budget
- the experience of being 'close to the customer' – both reflecting people's experience of current services, and providing an indicator of what new services are needed. While indices such as Acorn, Jarman and Townsend can provide a textbook measure of an area and its population, voluntary organisations will be able to provide a more up-to-date and accurate 'on the ground' picture
- a patchwork of different kinds of organisation: from major national to small community organisations
- for black and minority ethnic groups who are able to reflect the needs of their communities
- the opportunity to experiment and innovate. This toe-in-the-water approach is sometimes foreign to larger and more bureaucratic organisations, and allows a partnership to alter ways of working quickly to reflect immediate needs
- committed staff who are accustomed to being flexible and opportunistic. Staff are often attracted to work in the voluntary sector because of its more personal approach
- the experience of being 'users' of the health service – a consumeristic picture
- openness of information – voluntary organisations have a commitment to making complex information simple, and to being content to share it.

Why form a partnership to provide health promotion?

> 'Voluntary agencies are:
> 1. Concerned with the gaps and deficiencies in provision. They wouldn't be there otherwise.
> 2. Possessed of 'tunnel vision', that is their role.
> 3. Vehicles which often arise out of an individual, rather than a collective, vision.
> 4. Struggling to be born, to survive, to thrive and to grow constantly.
> 5. Almost by definition not capable of "being co-ordinated", they operate in the gaps and margins, and for every one brought into a co-ordinating net, more will spring to life because the gaps will always be there, and the individuals will always have the need to fill them and change things.
> All of this means that the voluntary sector often feels unmanageable, and unco-ordinateable. However, co-operation and collaboration are possible.'

THE OTHER PLAYERS - WHAT ROLE CAN THE STATUTORY AGENCIES HAVE?

The NHS is a highly professional machine. Its 40-plus years have created a system that is geared up to provide a high-technology service provision to a large population from the top down. It has a large structure already in place that radiates outwards, with its own designated locations which are perceived as having a health focus. It has long-term funding, resourcing and training, and its own distribution network. Lastly, it has a body of highly trained and dedicated staff.

Each of the constituent parts of the NHS has a possible partnership role to play; as have other statutory agencies. Here we look at possible (and actual) roles for the various 'actors':

(a) The Department of Health

The Department's role as a funder

Section 64 funding

> 'Funding and staffing are always a problem which fundamentally affects everything else.' (health information centre, serving self-help groups, North of England)

Section 64 of the Health Services and Public Health Act 1968 gives Department of Health Ministers the power to make grants to voluntary organisations. The Department runs several grant schemes but the two major ones, embracing all health and personal social service activity, are the Section 64 General Scheme and the Opportunities for Volunteering Scheme. The General Scheme is used mainly to core fund national voluntary organisations.

It also supports innovative national projects and local projects with a potential national significance.

The Opportunities for Volunteering Scheme is designed to provide opportunities for unemployed people to undertake voluntary service, and is administered by fifteen national voluntary organisations and a generalist consortium. These organisations reflect the interests of a wide variety of client groups in the health and personal social services field and act as the Department of Health's agents in distributing resources to local projects.

One example of the sort of health promotion project funded by Opportunities for Volunteering is Southwark Phoenix Women's Health Organisation, where funds, training facilities for staff and management, and supervision of the project, are provided by the Department. Southwark Phoenix, for its part, provides promotional material, volunteer training and support, counselling sessions, and distributes leaflets and videos on health issues. It aims 'to show women how to maintain good health, prevent illness, recognise early signs of illness and take the right steps towards restoring health again, in themselves or members of their family' (Southwark Women's Health Organisation leaflet for volunteer workers – Project 66).[3]

The Department also has a special programme to develop information on health and health services in minority ethnic languages. In the past, a number of innovative projects involving voluntary bodies have been funded out of this programme, such as: the London Chinese Health Resources Centre, the Royal College of Midwives Trust (funding to produce a booklet, *Choice and Rights in Maternity Care*); the Brook Advisory Centre (to fund a video *Having a Gynaecological Examination*), and a video and support material aimed at carers of Afro-Caribbean origin.

Detailed information on *all* funding offered by the Department of Health can be obtained from: Section 64 Funding Enquiries, Department of Health, Wellington House, 133–155 Waterloo Road, London SE1 8UG.

Regional and District Health Authorities also have delegated powers to award grants to voluntary organisations. It is for each region to determine the extent and nature of the funding they wish to make available to local voluntary groups.

> *'When we first started to research the project we visited the health authority where we were seen by the chairman and managing director. They were very pleasant to us, indicating that they liked our ideas but said that it was not possible to put them into practice at that time. They were delighted that we were volunteers (and fund-raisers) as this would not require them to lay out money!'* (co-ordinator of hospice project, South-east England)

The Department's strategic role

With the changes in the NHS, the role of the Department is also changing. With the devolution of power to Regional Health Authorities, the

Department's role will be to plan overall strategy, national targets and priorities, and leave the actual running of the service to Regions, and, less so, to Districts.

One example of the move away from central influence and control is the phasing out of *Health Circulars*, a traditional 'tool' which the Department used to prompt health authorities to carry out particular activities. This sort of centralised 'edict' appeared many times each year, on all sorts of issues, from purchasing to immunisation targets, and such a sea of paper was in danger of being ignored by a busy DHA.

These *Health Circulars* have sometimes been a bonus for voluntary organisations. For example, one circular, HC HN(90)10, issued by the Department in July 1990, aims to encourage District Health Authorities to develop local breastfeeding projects *in conjunction with a national voluntary organisation – the Joint Breastfeeding Initiative*. The circular offers particular guidance on ways in which this help may be given – DHAs are asked 'to encourage their maternity services liaison committees to publicise the Initiative and to hold training and other projects, and to agree study time for local Initiative projects'. The work of the Joint Breastfeeding Initiative is included in this report. See Appendix 2.

Managing the regions

In place of the central control, the management of a Regional Health Authority will be in the hands of a team of NHS managers, the NHS Executive, who will have the task of maintaining day-to-day contact with Regions.

Annually, the NHS Management Executive will sit down with each RHA and examine its plans for the year. While there is currently no specific direct instruction to Regions to form partnerships with voluntary organisations, one of the areas that *will* be scrutinised by the NHS Executive is the way in which an RHA makes use of all available resources at its disposal, which will include working with voluntary organisations in its area, as well as working with other agencies like the local authority.

(b) The Health Education Authority

The Health Education Authority is part of the NHS, and is designated a 'special' health authority, with the task of leading and supporting health education in this country. Note that it is the Health *Education* Authority and *not* the Health *Promotion* Authority. Its remit is

- to give information and advice about health directly to members of the public
- to support 'other health organisations, health professionals, and other people who provide health education to members of the public' (usually by providing resources and training)
- to advise government on matters related to health.[4]

The HEA's Strategic Plan 1990–95 is the HEA's charter for the way in which it will be working until 1995. Its role 'will continue to be mainly

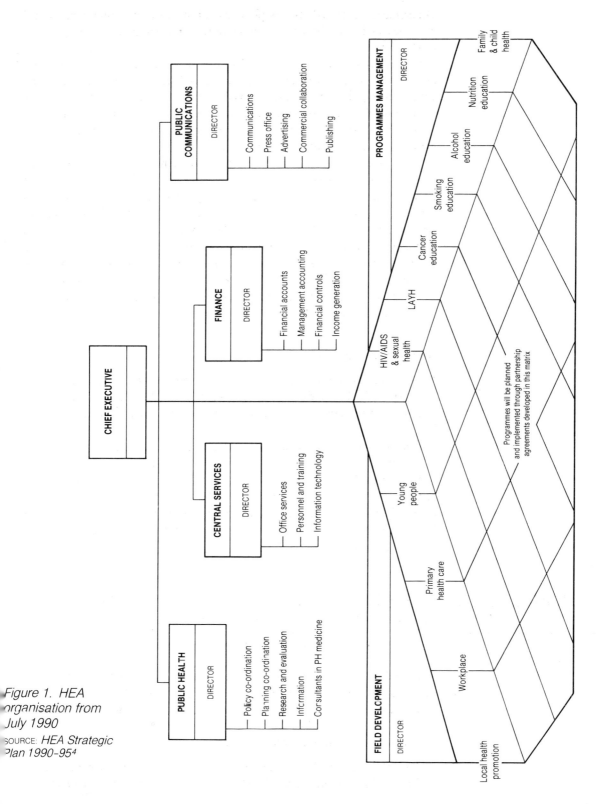

Figure 1. HEA
organisation from
July 1990
SOURCE: HEA Strategic
Plan 1990-95[4]

concerned with the promotion of good health and the prevention of disease', by prioritising a number of health programme areas. It has recently reorganised itself to integrate its services and to ensure that each programme area is carried out in the context of 'settings' in which health education may be delivered. This new 'matrix' approach is shown in Figure 1 and voluntary organisations should note that specific support is included for health promotion at a local level. This area of the Field Development Unit is an ideal initial point of contact for voluntary organisations seeking help and advice on any aspect of the HEA's work.

The HEA's strategic plan highlights the Authority's commitment to partnership as a way of working – not only with parts of the NHS, but with local authorities and with voluntary organisations. It recognises that 'the voluntary sector has considerable potential for health education through its links with local communities and groups, its support for self-help and advocacy of wider public health policies', and that there is a need 'to ensure that links between agencies (e.g. voluntary, local authority and sectors of industry) are strengthened and supported to stimulate and encourage the dissemination of effective practice'.[4]

Several of the HEA's programme areas are already actively involved in funding projects with voluntary organisations and community groups – for example, 270 community projects have been funded by the Look After Your Heart (LAYH) programme[5] at a cost of £700 000.

> 'We often work in partnership (as well as, at times, direct opposition!) with the health authority.' (women's health group)

(c) Regional and District Health Authorities

Regional Health Authorities

Under the new management system of the NHS, each of the fourteen Regional Health Authorities will be autonomous. They will be the agents for managing change within the NHS and ensuring the implementation of government policies, and will be strategically responsible for overseeing the process of establishing contracts, which ensure that local populations have access to a wide range of health services.

RHAs allocate resources to District Health Authorities and to Family Health Service Authorities, and monitor their performance in achieving agreed objectives. They are in turn managed by the NHS Executive. Regional Health Authorities can provide funding for voluntary organisations, and devise their own policy for doing so. Their strategic plan may include specific intentions of ways in which the Region plans to work with the voluntary sector in its area, and this document is a useful reference tool for voluntary organisations.

District Health Authorities

Many of the examples of partnership identified for this project are linked with District Health Authorities, some of whom are very active funders of local voluntary organisations. Many DHAs have laid down policies about working with the voluntary sector.

One example of this is Bristol and Weston Health Authority, which in 1989 carried out a survey of voluntary contribution to their work. Their policy statement 'recognises the extent, the importance and the value of voluntary effort in contributing to health care in the district', and job descriptions [of the unit administrators in each of the seven operational management units in the District] include the task of '. . . maintaining good relationships with the various voluntary bodies associated with the unit in conjunction with the District Voluntary Services Organiser, to foster a spirit of community involvement and voluntary service where appropriate in the unit'.[6] In Bristol and Weston the DHA employs a District Voluntary Services Organiser, with a small team of part-time assistants, who co-ordinate the work of individual volunteers in the area.

A new strategic role for District Health Authorities

In the restructured NHS, there is a split of tasks between 'purchasers' and 'providers'.

District Health Authorities now have a new key role as the main purchasers of health care. They will be responsible for ensuring that a comprehensive range of services is available to respond to health needs of their resident population and to local views on those services. There will be a very strong accent on 'knowing your market' – DHAs will 'seek to assess the health needs of their population' and they will then have to agree service contracts with provider units to purchase a full range of services which aim to meet these needs.

DHAs will be more conscious of looking for innovative options of delivering services, and will increasingly be looking outside the health services for other potential deliverers of services.

DHAs will also have to be more consumer responsive – to seek to identify the views of users of services and to act on them to make sure that services are delivered in ways which are more responsive to customer wishes. The Department of Health believes that this responsiveness will be achieved through the quality standards DHAs agree in their contracts with hospitals and other providers of care.

The DHA Project

To help DHAs enter this new climate of purchasing and contracting, the Department of Health has set up a development project team. This team is known as the DHA Project, or Project 26, and its work includes producing discussion documents, guidelines and offering advice to DHAs.

Although again there is no specific directive for DHAs to work with voluntary organisations, the team makes the point that DHAs are free to contract with any provider that they see fit, which can include voluntary organisations just as it can include any part of the NHS.

The key items will always be standards and quality of services, and if voluntary organisations can provide these, their services may be 'purchased' by DHAs. While there is no specific mention at present of 'accrediting' providers of services, this may evolve in years to come, simply as a means of helping DHAs to choose between potential providers of services. Voluntary organisations can find out more about the DHA Project by contacting: The DHA Project, NHS Management Executive, Room G14, Richmond House, London SW1A 2NS.

(d) Health promotion units

There is much discussion among health professionals on the overlap between health education and health promotion. For simplicity, we have referred throughout this report to health promotion units (and officers, and other similar workers), assuming the term also to include health education units.

Health promotion units now

> 'There has already been discerned a general enthusiasm for closer working among all those groups, individuals, agencies and organisations which have a "health input". The obstacles are the ongoing problem of professional jealousies and the traditional approaches to health promotion which view it as a single profession, rather than as a community-based initiative.' (local council health development officer)

Health promotion units have until now been sited within the NHS structure, within District Health Authorities, accountable to Directors of Public Health. It is currently generally accepted that the health promotion service of each health authority has the lead role in initiating, co-ordinating and supporting health education/health promotion activity. It is also accepted that the *precise* role and relationship is a matter for District Health Authorities and will vary according to approach and needs.

Health promotion units currently typically consist of approximately five health promotion specialists and a number of clerical or other support services. A small number of units are currently much larger than this, with up to twenty specialists on the staff. Units have non-staff budgets ranging from approximately £10 000 to £50 000. In 1990 there were approximately 800 health promotion specialists in the UK, according to a report by the King's Fund Institute.[7]

The role of the health promotion officer

The role of the health promotion officer is 'to promote the health of the local population by enabling people to increase control over and improve their health', and the functions of health promotion units are:

- to translate national HE/HP guidelines to ensure they meet local planning needs and are implemented accordingly
- to assess local needs together with Directors of Public Health and other health professionals within the health authority, and in collaboration with voluntary and statutory organisations representing the community
- to input into the formulation of District HA policy – including to operational and strategic planning
- to manage HE/HP programmes to address specific issues (e.g. AIDS) or based on population needs (e.g. needs of minority ethnic groups)
- to provide advice and consultation – to the public and to policy-makers (in both statutory and voluntary bodies)
- to provide training and support to all health educators.[8]

The Society of Health Education and Health Promotion Officers has defined the following indicators for what it believes a 'good quality' health promotion department should offer:

- it should have a clearly defined role based on the systematic assessment of health needs of the local population (which should go beyond the assessment of epidemiological data by taking into account the needs of the local community)
- it should offer a strategic approach, encompassing health programmes based on key groups and key settings within the community, each programme having measurable targets
- its programmes should utilise the full range of health promotion methods/approaches
- health promotion strategies should reflect a number of key health promotion principles embodied in Health for All 2000:

  - equity, both in health status and service provision
  - intersectoral collaboration
  - community participation
  - the role of advocacy and empowerment
  - emphasis to be placed on the importance of efficiency, effectiveness and economy in the planning, delivery and evaluation of health promotion initiatives.

Parkside Health Promotion Unit, in North London, is an example of a unit which believes strongly in working across boundaries and in finding innovative solutions to health promotion problems. Parkside is probably unique in that it has been working with community health service staff, to develop their skills and experience to work in community-oriented ways, for over ten years.

These years cover its history, first under Kensington, Chelsea and Westminster Health Authorities, and then under Paddington and North Kensington and Brent Health Authorities. Its efforts are regarded as a 'pioneering' example in the field of health promotion, and many consider it to be a model of its kind in its approach to dealing with voluntary groups and the community.

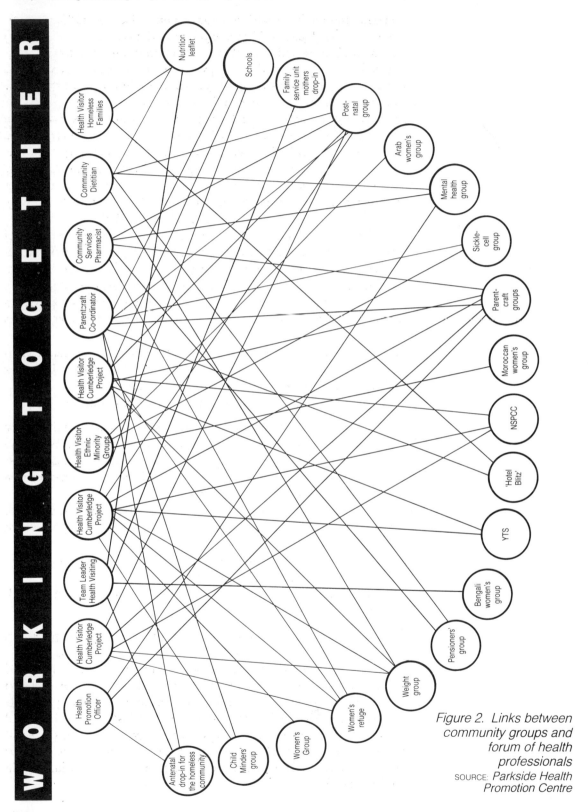

Figure 2. Links between
community groups and
forum of health
professionals
SOURCE: Parkside Health
Promotion Centre

Parkside was the first health promotion unit to have, in 1980, a specific Community Development Health Education Officer, who was a health visitor with a background of developing links with community groups.[9] Jean Spray and Karen Greenwood have documented the milestones over the first ten years in 'The progress of a community development approach in one health district: from street work to District policy'.[9]

First was the appointment, in 1983, of a health visitor whose brief was to 'examine how a health visitor can work within existing community groups to promote awareness of health issues'. Vari Drennan, the health visitor, made contact with 40 different voluntary groups within the community, working closely with 23 of them. The results of her work, and analysis of the issues and difficulties involved are contained in *Working in a Different Way* published by Parkside Health Promotion Unit in 1985.[10]

In 1988, Parkside HPU convened the Community Forum – a forum of health professionals from health visiting, midwifery, pharmacy and dietetics in the district who were all employed in posts which allowed them space to develop their work practice in new and creative ways. Members of the forum met to develop a programme of professional support and development to enable them to reorientate their services to meet the needs of the communities in which they worked.

Through the forum the members worked together to foster partnerships with community groups in the area. Figure 2 shows the numerous links that exist between forum members and community groups.

Examples of the partnerships with voluntary groups illustrated were:

- work with homeless families in Bayswater: the Bayswater Families Care Team including health visitors, social workers and welfare workers (funded from joint funding), and the Bayswater Project, a voluntary organisation providing advice and help to families in bed and breakfast accommodation including advice on access to health services
- work with the Moroccan Women's Group to help address and overcome cultural problems that Moroccan women encountered when using the Health Service.

See *Working Together: Innovations in Work for Primary Health Care* from Parkside Health Promotion Unit.[11]

The unit itself is also involved in fostering current partnerships with community groups in the area, for example:

- 'Throwing Stones' – a young people's theatre/health promotion project on HIV/AIDS, run in conjunction with the Royal Court Young People's Theatre in London. Young people were recruited through the local Employment Training Scheme, and took part in a series of workshops on HIV/AIDS jointly run with the health promotion unit. The young people developed acting skills, and, with a script writer, devised a play which toured local schools, youth and community centres, and was put on at the Royal Court Theatre Upstairs. This project has been so successful that a similar two-year project has been funded to develop HIV and sex education in secondary schools.

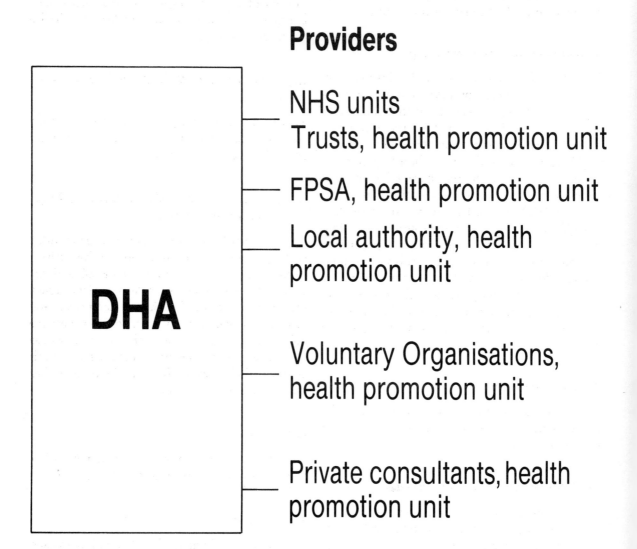

Providers

DHA

NHS units
Trusts, health promotion unit

FPSA, health promotion unit

Local authority, health
promotion unit

Voluntary Organisations,
health promotion unit

Private consultants, health
promotion unit

*Figure 3. The option of a
combination of agencies
supplying the functions
of health promotion
departments*
SOURCE: *Health Promotion in
the 1990s* [15]

Organisation

DHA has or buys in health promotion advice. Health promotion is provided by a range of agencies with whom the DHA may, or not, contract.

Implications for health promotion

Very difficult for co-ordination of a District, city-wide strategy of health promotion in these circumstances. A strong purchasing function for health promotion would be required to ensure that contracted agencies co-ordinated their work. Many DHA units have little or no health promotion expertise at present. This may have to be funded or provided by current health promotion team being split up. HEPS would have to become generalists and effectiveness would suffer. Professionals would, perhaps, be isolated unless health promotion forums existed. There would probably be no central resource for research, evaluation, training, policy development available, therefore these aspects are likely to suffer. Health promotion within units may be strengthened where there was little previous health promotion work.

Funding implications

Likely to cost more as more expertise would be needed within provider units. This option may split scarce resources.

Strategies needed for effective working

District-wide forums for health promotion specialists to meet together for support and co-ordination. Very efficient and effective planning and contracting functions at DHA level. Excellent inter-agency collaboration. Strong commitment by all provider units, organisations to the health promotion function.

Implications for health needs assessment

Mechanisms would be needed that allowed health promotion within provider units to have a view of the health promotion needs of the population. Research strategies with HEPS involvement may be difficult to co-ordinate. However, health promotion expertise within organisations/units may enable more grass roots research to feed into health needs assessment processes.

Implications for Health for All and intersectoral work

This would be extremely difficult without a strong co-ordinating team. It may lead to greater emphasis on HFA targets over principles.

Implications for inter Health Authority working, and national collaboration

It would be difficult for DHA provider units with a health promotion function to work collaboratively across district boundaries. In terms of national collaboration it is uncertain how national funds would be allocated for district campaigns and activities, or who would be the contact with the HEA. Units/organisations within a district would compete for national health promotion funds yet all be doing similar work. It would be possible that there would be duplication.

Other issues

It is likely that there would be no overall lead or direction for health promotion within a District.

Recommendations

This option would need a lot of co-ordination and planning, built up over a long period of time. It could lead to increased health promotion activities at all levels if well resourced. However, the quality of such activity would need careful monitoring. Inter-agency work is difficult to develop where there is a strong co-ordinating team – without such a team then the ability of this option to deliver a co-ordinated, inter-agency strategy for health promotion must be seriously questioned.

Similarly Lewisham and North Southwark Health Promotion Unit have a health promotion officer whose task is liaison with community groups:

> All the work undertaken within the remit of this post involves a partnership of one kind or another. We have contact with a wide range of organisations and groups within the community sector in the local area. We give support to the groups in producing their own health education resource materials; encouraging groups to use existing resources and creating opportunities for groups to come together when they have common interests and concerns.
>
> Recent and current examples of partnerships are: planning a series of health days for older people to give them an opportunity to express their health needs and problems. The co-ordinating group included representatives of local pensioners' groups and workers from local voluntary organisations, local authorities and the health authority; membership of a group looking at the health needs of the Bengali community in a particular local area of North Southwark. Members of the group include members of the local Bengali community, local community workers, local health visitors, health service administrator, community health council representative.[12]

The future

At the time of writing this report (October 1990) health promotion departments were entering an era of change. With the NHS re-organisation, and the accent on a 'purchaser' and 'provider' structure, health promotion units will be in the somewhat strange position of being both purchaser and provider.

The reporting line is changing too. At that time it was estimated that 50 per cent or more of health promotion departments are no longer accountable to Directors of Public Health, and that in a year's time, even fewer will be.[13]

Project 26 (see above) has also looked at the role of health promotion departments, and analysed the dual roles that health promotion units will have:

Purchaser activities will include:

- investigating health needs
- advice on health policies, goals and objectives
- reviewing contracts
- co-ordination of plans and activities between different agencies.

Provider-type activities might include:

- planning and evaluation of health promotion programmes
- provision of networks for communication between staff, DHAs and the local community and for community participation
- provision of training, advice and health promotion materials/resources for health professionals and staff working in other agencies (for example, schools, voluntary sector) and community leaders
- direct education and advice to members of the public
- influencing key opinion formers.[14]

Given the number of roles that health promotion units may have, one of

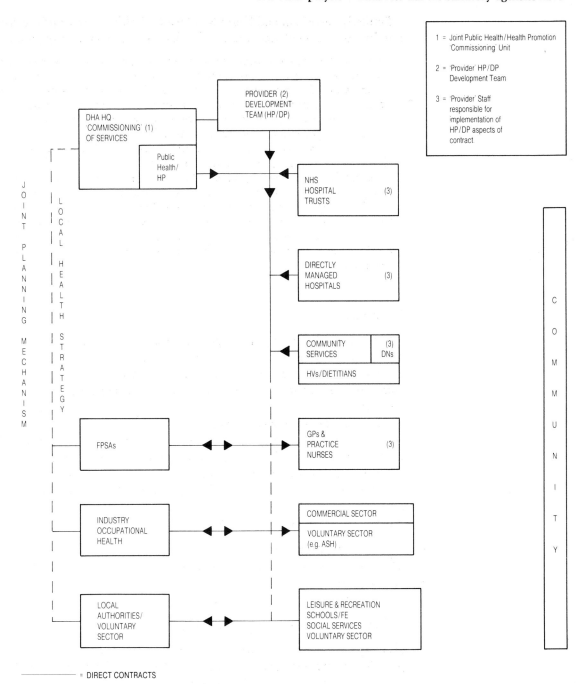

Figure 4. *Organisation of health promotion/ disease prevention services*
SOURCE: *HEA discussion paper* [16]

the options being considered for the future is that the traditional functions of health promotion departments may be provided by a combination of different agencies, including the voluntary sector as well as the health promotion unit. This option is shown in more detail in Figure 3, an extract from *Health Promotion in the 1990s*,[15] and in Figure 4, from a Health Education Authority discussion paper.[16] There is a real role for voluntary organisations, but, as the document notes, the greatest difficulty perhaps will be one of co-ordinating the different agencies involved.

(e) The Family Health Service Authorities

FHSAs replace the old Family Practitioner Committees. They will be accountable to RHAs for managing the services provided by the primary care team in contract with the NHS. This primary care team includes the GP, health visitor, practice nurse, plus the community services team – the district nurse, community, psychiatric nurse, physiotherapists, speech therapists, dietitians, and midwives. There are also other services which interact directly with the community – for example, the dentist, optician, pharmacist, and chiropodist.

FHSAs already have links with Community Health Councils (see below), and many already have their own links with local voluntary agencies, such as the Council for Voluntary Service and Rural Community Councils.

The Society of Family Practitioner Committees will cease to exist, and individual FHSAs will have the opportunity instead to join the National Association of Health Authorities and Trusts (NAHAT).

In collaboration with the DHAs, FHSAs will assess the health needs of the population and ensure that services are targeted effectively. They will plan provision of services in the context of national contracts, and manage the contracts (and the budgets) of smaller groups of GPs, dentists, pharmacists and opticians. They will also now have a specific directive to provide health promotion for their patients.

The primary care team and health promotion

> 'Our major obstacle has been the total failure of the midwifery service to give value to the work done by the community midwife based within the project. The result of this was that the midwife was transferred to another area without warning and a midwife without any experience or understanding of community work replaced her. This has led to conflict within the project and women leaving the project to the extent that it has become a management issue ... which has not been overcome'. (parents' support group particularly concerned with pregnant women and young children)

Various parts of the primary care team are involved in health promotion activities. Many health visitors are involved in community projects (see the example of Parkside Health Promotion Unit, pp. 23–5), and although much of dentists', opticians' and pharmacists' work is 'service provision', there is often a health promotion element. For example, apart from providing blood pressure and cholesterol measurement, pregnancy testing and needle exchange services, pharmacists also offer advice on the treatment of minor ailments, and on using and storing medicines. Pharmacists are involved in various pilot schemes being carried out in conjunction with voluntary organisations such as Age Concern over the recording of drug prescription for elderly and confused patients, and under the re-organisation of the NHS can now claim a fee from the FHSA for organising such initiatives.

Health promotion and GPs

The GP is the front line of the Health Service with the consumer, and is being given a specific role to play in health promotion by the new NHS contract. GPs are now being funded by FHSAs to provide three kinds of one-to-one health promotion check:

- a check for the over-75s – the cost of which is covered by the increased capitation payment a GP receives for someone over 75 who is registered with the practice. (This may not always be carried out by the GP – sometimes it is done by the practice nurse, or someone specially employed. The Helen Hamlyn Research Unit at St Mary's Hospital in Paddington, London, is training linkworkers to carry out a structured assessment using a portable computer, and reporting back to the GP.[17] Under this scheme there is no requirement for the linkworker to have a specific professional qualification.)
- an initial health check on registration of a new patient over 5 (for which the GP will be financially reimbursed by the FHSA)
- a three-yearly health check for anyone between the ages of 16 and 74 registered with the practice, who has not been seen by the GP during that time.

Other GP health promotion clinics

In addition to the checks mentioned above, GPs will now be able to claim a fee from their FHSA for any clinics that they run which qualify as 'health promotion' clinics. (The health promotion fee for 10 patients – after 1 January 1991 – will be £45.)[18]

Because FHSAs are autonomous, each area has its own interpretation of what may constitute a 'health promotion' clinic. This represents a real opportunity for voluntary organisations, for individual FHSAs will now be able to authorise payment to GPs who are using voluntary organisations to run specific clinics for them, *providing* the GP can convince the FHSA that the clinic provided is a high quality health promotion clinic, run by 'suitably qualified' people.

Again, there is latitude for individual FHSAs to interpret the words 'suitably qualified' in the exact way they wish. There is no statutory obligation for anyone involved in health promotion to have a particular qualification, and the qualifications accepted by GPs (and FHSAs) will vary – in one area, for example, the local FHSA already authorises GPs to use volunteers who have a qualification in counselling to run clinics.

Examples of the types of clinics in which voluntary organisations could be involved include stress-management clinics, well-person, diabetes, heart disease, anti-smoking, alcohol control, as well as those where there is an emphasis on counselling.

How to convince GPs of the value of working in partnership with the voluntary sector?

It is rare to find a GP surgery without an enthusiastic display of addresses and information about local voluntary organisations on its notice board. But besides voluntary organisations potentially becoming involved in health promotion clinics, can other partnerships be fostered between GPs and voluntary organisations?

As one project puts it,

> Our GPs are not aware of the services which the project provides, which they themselves could make use of – for example, our newsletter. The GPs have complained to the project about low take-up of preventive services such as immunisations, cervical smears, etc., and this may provide an entry point for the project to begin to communicate regularly.

> Given the high social needs on the ——— Estate, it is likely that many patients consult GPs about conditions which are directly or indirectly related to their personal circumstances. These circumstances might include poor housing, unemployment, poverty or relationship difficulties and inevitably it will be the symptoms of these problems that are treated at the surgery . . .

> Our project offers people help to identify their collective health needs and to identify what they feel needs to change or to be provided in order to help them maintain good health. The project, along with local people, has been involved in providing many of these services. It has also worked closely with professionals to help them to provide their services in a way which is more sensitive to local needs . . . It is important that the GPs begin to realise the potential of the project.

Why do some GPs appear reluctant to use the services of voluntary organisations? Is it that the concept of 'partnership' outside the accepted relationship of the practice may be difficult for the GP to grasp? Dr Joan Lennard, the Royal College of GPs representative on the Project Advisory Group believes that this could be one reason: ' "partnership" is a legal and binding term, covering certain required patterns of behaviour and the distribution of income earned as a result of that partnership'.

She continues,

> Perhaps GPs need to understand better that working in partnership with voluntary services really means working in close co-operation with them, recognising their worth, and utilising the contributions to the workload that they offer.

> The reverse of this coin is that voluntary services working with the patients of GPs need to communicate back to the GPs about the work done – even if just listening, which is often so vital – and letting the GPs know when this contact with a given patient ends. Many GPs will not use voluntary services because there is no feedback, so that if the GP refers the patient it looks as though she is passing the

buck, and is not interested. Our local marriage guidance counsellor (at the local health centre) was quite excellent in ringing us, and letting us know how things were going.[19]

Successful partnerships with GPs

There are successful health promotion partnerships between GPs and voluntary organisations. Here are several examples:

(a) Primary care facilitators

Over the last six years, many FHSAs and health authorities have funded the post of primary care facilitator within their areas. This post began initially because of involvement by a voluntary organisation, the Chest, Heart and Stroke Association. Primary care facilitators were the brainchild of a research project, the Oxford Prevention of Heart Attack and Stroke Project, which believed there was a role for the nurse to carry out health promotion in GPs' surgeries – typically, the taking of blood pressure and providing advice on how to fight heart disease. The facilitator, who is generally a nurse with a primary health care background, acts as a district-wide catalyst and resource to practices to extend their preventive medicine programme. The Chest, Heart and Stroke Association funded the first six trial practices in 1982 and has continued, along with the HEA and the Department of Health, to provide funding. Primary care facilitators are seen as an important health promotion initiative, and have now been appointed in 150 health districts covering a total of 37 million of the population.

(b) Health First

Health First is a local networking group which 'focuses on effective methods of promoting health in a low-income area', based at a GP practice in Baits Green Health Centre, Norwich.

The project was originally started in 1988 by the wife of one of the GPs with funding from Norwich City Council. The practice has seven GPs, based on three sites, and is also a base for health visitors and district nurses. The practice provides the rent-free accommodation for Health First, and it is hoped in the future to have a door which opens on to the street, giving direct access to the public.

The majority of people seen are referred by the primary care team, via the weekly practice meetings, which a representative from Health First attends, but there are self-referrals too. The referred case is then visited at home or is invited to the health centre. There, Health First aims to help them identify their particular difficulties and then supports them in finding out further information, joining a support group, finding further training, etc.

Health First itself says of its work:

We offer help for health in a non-medical way; we offer information and support on a range of social problems, and access to specialist help and facilities which are often out of reach of low-income communities . . . The GPs and primary care team use the helpline resource and find it very helpful in offering alternative options, e.g. education, training, help with benefits; help with childcare, etc. – not pills.[20]

Although the philosophy is to refer people to existing groups, rather than forming new ones, various new groups have been initiated or supported: a nutrition group, which offers advice on healthy eating; two slimming groups (which look at holistic ways of losing weight); and the 'Coffee Break' group. All the groups have crèche facilities – paid for either by the practice or by the social services department.

(c) Patient participation groups

Some GPs have set up 'patient participation groups' (PPGs). This is the concept of having a supportive group of patients, and at bottom it is the belief that 'patients, doctors and other medical staff can work together to develop the provision of health services and to realise health care goals'. The concept first took off in 1972/73, and there are now approximately 300 PPGs up and down the country. The Association of Patient Participation Groups has noticed a significant increase of interest with the NHS changes and new GP contracts, where there is a greater emphasis on patient information.

All patients registered with the practice are eligible to attend meetings and elect a committee. Most committees are chaired by a patient, and the activities of a particular PPG may fall into any or all of three categories: community care, health education, and feedback to the practice. Examples of additional facilities achieved by PPGs include a transport system, prescription delivery services for the housebound, crèche facilities, patients' libraries, as well as fund-raising for the practice to buy new equipment.

(The National Association for Patient Participation can be contacted through their honorary secretary, at 50 Wallasey Village, Wallasey, Merseyside L45 3ML. The association will be happy to provide information for anyone wishing to set up a PPG.)

(f) Community Health Councils

Community Health Councils (CHCs) were set up in 1974 by Act of Parliament to represent the interests of patients and the community to managers of the Health Service. There are currently 215 Community Health Councils in England and Wales, financed by allocation of funds from Regional Health Authorities. CHCs are usually composed of around 18 members, who are a mix of statutory and voluntary members.

Typically, CHCs respond to changes in local health services; carry out surveys of local health facilities and patient satisfaction. CHCs have a duty to monitor local services and must be consulted on changes in health care provision. They produce information guides and provide independent advice for local people; highlight unmet need and campaign for improvements to local services. They also meet and make links with other local community groups and voluntary organisations and take up issues raised by local groups of users, representing these groups to the health authority. CHCs encourage community participation in their work and hold regular meetings with the public to keep in touch with the health concerns of the local community.

CHCs are involved in many different kinds of partnerships throughout the country, which are regularly documented in their annual reports, and vary from joint policy-making partnerships to production of local health guides and directories. However, one particularly innovative project is currently being carried out by Newcastle CHC, which have been the catalyst in developing the Newcastle Healthy Cities project partnership (see Appendix 2, pp. 89–90 for more about the UK Health for All Network).

Newcastle CHC held a conference in collaboration with Newcastle CVS, with the express purpose of helping the voluntary sector to develop its 'vision' for this project. Once this had been refined, the CHC approached the statutory sector to secure partners for funding, which produced:

- a grant from the Baring Foundation
- a grant and support from the District Health Authority
- a limited amount of money from Newcastle local authority.

In setting up the Newcastle Healthy Cities project, the CHC have used as a model the partnership that exists within the CHC structure – that is, a mix of members of the local commercial community, the university, the local authority and the District Health Authority, as well as members of voluntary organisations. This group will eventually take over the project and will nominate a management group to run the project on a day-to-day basis. The group has also applied for individual funding status – it has its own constitution and is applying for charitable status. Newcastle CHC are hopeful that the move to involve members of the local business community will be of particular benefit – once they are a registered charity – in attracting further funding.

(g) Other government departments

Many government departments are involved in partnerships with voluntary bodies, for example, the Department of Transport, Department of the Environment, the Home Office, and the Department of Education and Science.

'Obstacles: difficulties in being employed by statutory bodies - overtones of authority, difficulties in feeding back "bottom-up" suggestions through a bureaucracy' (ex-project worker on community health project - project now terminated because of expiry of funding)

(h) Local authorities

Local authorities – with their involvement in health and social issues, are already very active in partnerships with the voluntary sector, as will be seen from the examples quoted below. Many projects receive funding through Joint Funding/Joint Consultative Committees (jointly between health authority and local authority).

Social Services Departments already provide most non-hospital day care services. The Association of County Councils recently found that between 0.5 and 9.8 per cent of social services budgets were being channelled through voluntary organisations on an agency basis, with Age Concern England being aware of over 30 local branches being involved in negotiating contracts for the provision of major services.[21] Even parish councils, possibly the lowest rung of authority, are often some of the most actively involved in partnerships with voluntary agencies, particularly in rural areas.

Local authority Environmental Health Departments

Environmental Health Departments are one of the few departments within local authorities with 'health' in their title. Some have developed extensive contacts and ways of working with voluntary organisations. One example is Leicester's local authority health promotion unit, based within the Environmental Health Department. Their objectives are:

- to achieve equity in health, and to reduce differences in the current health status of people in Leicester
- to ensure equal opportunities to enable all people in Leicester to achieve their full health potential.

The unit has developed a number of initiatives involving working 'in partnership' on areas that are perceived by them to be high priority in the Leicestershire area: black and minority ethnic issues, women's health, and HIV/AIDS.

The unit has a special 'small grants' budget (£10000 in the current financial year), and community projects are encouraged to apply for grants of up to £2000. Information and help is available from the unit on how to put in a formal approach for funding.

Leicester is keen to support and empower voluntary organisations, and to provide help in understanding how a statutory body works. They have offered local voluntary organisations advice on organisational skills, access to equipment, and use of what is known within the department as 'the voluntary desk'. This is a free desk in the unit which is assigned to a developing voluntary group which may not have its own premises elsewhere. One particular group member is given the use of the desk for various periods of time each week, and has the opportunity of becoming part of the health promotion unit, and understanding how the unit works and the demands made on its time and personnel.

Sandra Whiles, Health Promotion Manager, meets informally with the voluntary 'guest' to discuss any matters arising and offer help and resolve problems. So far, a range of voluntary organisations have used the desk since it was set up in 1988, and feedback has been very positive from both the voluntary organisation, and from other members of the health promotion team.

Local education authorities

Local education authorities are becoming involved in partnerships with voluntary organisations. One example is the work being done in the London Borough of Newham with Newham Alcohol Advisory Service on producing education material for local schools on the subject of alcohol education and misuse prevention.

The corporate world offers tremendous potential for partnership, although most often their role is a financial one, providing small- to medium-scale project-related funding. However, some companies are involved in both using the workplace as a 'setting' for health promotion (and providing health promotion for their own staff), and providing healthy choices for their customers.

Health promotion for staff

The strategic plan of the HEA's Look After Your Heart programme has specific targets for employers:

> employers will be encouraged to look after their workers' health by introducing a wide range of activities into the workplace, including smoking policies, healthy eating policies, promotion of physical activity, health checks and LAYH:LAY (Look After Yourself) classes. The aim by 1995 will be to involve workplaces employing 6 million employees (about 30 per cent of the nation's total workforce.[22]

There are many examples of mobile health and fitness exhibitions for both staff and customers: the Coronary Prevention Group's Heart Health Programme was set up with a grant from BP. It provides health promotion services in the workplace by bringing in a team of four CPG staff, two nurses, a dietitian and a health promotion officer, who take employees through a range of measures designed to illustrate their risk of heart disease and how they can take action to reduce that risk. So far, CPG have worked with a wide range of companies, including London Transport and Esso Petroleum. They plan to extend the programme to bring their services to schools and the public.

The Chest, Heart and Stroke Association runs a 'human MOT' scheme, similar to that offered in GPs' surgeries by the primary health care facilitators. This mobile stand has been exhibited in airports, railways stations, racecourses and town centres, and, like the CPG's stand, includes blood pressure monitoring kit and advice on lifestyle and diet. Kwik-Save Supermarkets, who chose the Chest, Heart and Stroke Association as their charity for 1989/90, celebrate openings of new supermarkets by mounting the exhibition in store, to test both customers and staff.

In addition, registered charities like the London Hazards Centre maintain a continuing interest in occupational injuries, such as repetitive strain injury, VDU usage, and 'sick building syndrome', and regularly issue publications and offer advice on these subjects.

Health promotion with customers

Many of the 'healthier food' producers and retailers are involved in co-promotions with the Look After Your Heart programme, organised by the HEA. This comes under the umbrella title of 'Look after Your Customer'; for example, the Hull Healthy City Initiative (see case study in Appendix 2, pp. 90–4) has been actively involved with Grandway Supermarkets (a local chain) in developing a 'healthy shopping basket'.

The ethics of receiving funding from the corporate sector

In recent years, the commercial sector has become a heavy funder of voluntary organisations. Companies mentioned in questionnaires included IBM, the local electricity board, who partly-sponsor the Nottingham Self-Help Team, helping to support almost 200 self-help groups in the Nottinghamshire area, and Allied Dunbar, who support Health Matters in Swindon, an independent voluntary organisation working with people who are carers or involved with self-help support groups.

Ethical considerations often only arise when support from the corporate sector comes less out of corporate altruism and more out of public relations needs, when strings are attached. A growing number of voluntary organisations in the health sector will not accept moneys offered by companies in sectors that produce health 'hazards' – for example, drink and tobacco, or from pharmaceutical companies.

The European perspective

Health matters to Europe. The Community Charter for Fundamental Social Rights for Workers emphasises an obligation to look after the health of workers throughout Europe, and the European Social Fund is a potential source of specialist funding for voluntary organisations. The Europe Against Cancer Programme is an example of one area where specific health promotion targets have been laid down. Here the aim is to reduce mortality from cancer in Europe by 15 per cent between now and the year 2000.

In the field of heart disease, the International Heart Network (IHN) is a group of more than 70 individuals and non-governmental organisations throughout the world, committed to the prevention of cardiovascular diseases. The European Community Office (IHN–ECO) is part of this larger network, and has been developed by organisations in EC countries which are committed to tackling cardiovascular disease – for example, the Coronary Prevention Group, the British Heart Foundation and the Northern Ireland Chest, Heart and Stroke Association are all members. IHN–ECO gathers information on EC initiatives which will affect cardiovascular disease and the risk factors associated with its development; ensures that members are kept informed of relevant EC proposals and activities; co-ordinates responses to EC initiatives and generally promotes the heart–health perspective throughout the EC's consultative process.[23]

NOTES AND REFERENCES

1 *Relationships between Volunteers and Paid Non-professional Workers.* Volunteer Centre, Berkhamsted, 1975 (available from the Volunteer Centre, 29 Lower Kings Road, Berkhamsted, Herts., price 50p).

2 *Effectiveness and the Voluntary Sector*, Report of a Working Party established by NCVO. NCVO, 1990.

3 Southwark Women's Health Organisation – leaflet for volunteer workers, 1990.

4 *Health Education Authority: Strategic Plan 1990–95*. HEA, 1990.

5 *Heart Disease in the 1990s: a Strategy for 1990–95*. HEA, 1990.

6 Bristol and Weston Health Authority, Survey of Voluntary Contribution to the Work of the Health Authority, 1990.

7 King's Fund Institute. *Health Promotion in the 1990s: Organisational Options for Health Promotion Services*. Society of Health Education and Health Promotion Officers, 1990 (available, price £8, from the Society of Health Education and Health Promotion Officers, 11 Portland Square, Carlisle, Cumbria CA1 1PY).

8 *Consensus Workshop Report*. Society of Health Education and Health Promotion Officers, 1990.

9 Jean Spray and Karen Greenwood, 'The progress of a community development approach in one health district: from street work to District policy' in C. J. Martin, and D. V. McQueen (eds) *Readings for a New Public Health*. Edinburgh University Press, 1989.

10 Vari Drennan, *Working in a Different Way*. Parkside Health Promotion Unit, 1985 (available from Parkside Health Promotion Unit, Green Lodge, Barretts Green Road, London NW10 7AP, price £3.50).

11 *Working Together: Innovations in Work for Primary Health Care*. Parkside Health Promotion Unit (available from Parkside Health Promotion Unit, Green Lodge, Barretts Green Road, London NW10 7AP, price £3).

12 Report from Lewisham and North Southwark Health Promotion Department, June 1990.

13 J. French, Secretary of the Society of Health Education and Health Promotion Officers, personal communication, 1990.

14 Project 26, paper by Pat Troop, Director of Public Health, Cambridge Health Authority, June 1990.

15 King's Fund Institute. *Health Promotion in the 1990s: Organisational Options for Health Promotion Services*. Society of Health Education and Health Promotion Officers, 1990 (available, price £8, from the Society of Health Education and Health Promotion Officers, 11 Portland Square, Carlisle, Cumbria CA1 1PY).

16 *Implications for Health Promotion/Disease Prevention* (HEA discussion paper). Health Education Authority, 1990.

17 North Kensington Elderly People's Integrated Care Scheme (NKEPICS), c/o The Helen Hamlin Research Unit, Department of General Practice, St Mary's Hospital Medical School, Norfolk Place, London W2 1PG.

18 Association of Community Health Councils of England and Wales (ASCHCE&W), 30 Drayton Park, London N5 1PB.

19 Dr J. Lennard, personal communication.

20 Health First, communication to project worker.

21 *New Times, New Challenges*. NCVO, 1989.

22 *Beating Heart Disease in the 1990s: a Strategy for 1990–95*. HEA, 1990.

23 IHN–ECO leaflet. Contact IHN–ECO Secretariat through Jeanette Longfield, c/o Coronary Prevention Group, 102 Gloucester Place, London W1H 3DA.

4 PARTNERSHIPS – THE PRACTICE

Partnerships developing in the following areas were identified:

1 Training
2 Campaigning and advocacy
3 Access
4 Self-help
5 Information and education
6 Policy development
7 Service provision.

Brief details of the partnerships follow.

The balance of strength

The balance of strength in the partnerships varied from one extreme to the other. At one end, and often very common, are pure funding-only partnerships. This is usually a situation where the voluntary group is applying to the statutory partner for money or resources (for instance, office accommodation), and then goes away and 'gets on with the job'. It would almost be better to call these 'arrangements' rather than partnerships, because the relationship is very one-sided, with the voluntary sector partner often adopting a 'cap in hand' attitude.

Occasionally the voluntary sector is the lead funder, or key fund-raiser, appreciated for providing moneys the NHS cannot. An example of this is the Walsall Mastectomy and Breast Cancer Support Group. In April 1984:

> [We] set up a special fund to establish a dedicated chemotherapy unit staffed with highly trained nurses, at the Walsall and District General (Manor) Hospital . . . at present patients requiring chemotherapy have to be treated in a general ward among patients having treatment for a variety of conditions. This situation can be very distressing for all patients on such a ward. Thanks to the hard work of members, friends and various groups of people from the local community, our 'Chemotherapy Fund' has reached the magnificent total of £73 000 (as at May 1990), and we haven't finished yet![1]

The second type of partnership might commonly involve both funding and personnel – where moneys and part of staff time (for example, part of the workload of a health visitor) is provided by the Health Service, and the voluntary sector provides the management structure, premises and other volunteers as support workers.

Thirdly, there is a more equal relationship, where workloads and team objectives have to be discussed and shared.

And finally, there is what we believe to be a real joint working: where each side of the partnership has an input into both policy and day-to-day staffing and running conditions. While in this situation it is still more likely that the funding will be coming from the Health Service partner, there is real potential for each side to grow within the equation.

1. Training

(a) Wandsworth Volunteer Bureau – funded by the local authority to utilise volunteers as experienced health workers

Over the last few years Wandsworth Volunteer Bureau has become increasingly involved in working with volunteers who have experienced mental health, drug or alcohol-related problems, recognising 'that these individuals offer a valuable and under-developed resource for the community'. Wandsworth Volunteer Bureau (through the role of Development Worker for Mental Health) aims to develop opportunities for voluntary work in the borough for people who have experience of mental health, drug or related problems. 'We believe it will also counteract the negative stereotypes of the mentally ill, and promote self-esteem and confidence in volunteers', the bureau says. The Volunteer Bureau provides office premises, management committee, supervision, administration and liaison, and there is joint funding from Wandsworth Council and Wandsworth Health Authority. (Project No. 132)

(b) Outset – a voluntary organisation working in partnership with the health authority to develop a partnership to provide training and office skills

Outset is a registered charity established in 1970 and 'backed by investment from private and public sources to provide expertise in disability and employment'. It has just begun to implement a partnership with the Community and Mental Health Services Unit of South Bedfordshire Health Authority to provide 'opportunities in the community for people with mental health problems' via a rehabilitation project which includes information technology-based training and rehabilitation and placements in a new office bureau. (Project No. 134)

(c) Chiltern and Wycombe Volunteer Bureaux – working with the health authority to meet specific training needs

The Chiltern and Wycombe Volunteer Bureaux in conjunction with Wycombe Health Authority are offering training courses for voluntary workers and health care professionals involved in the care of the terminally ill. The voluntary sector has been given six places on each course. Trainers from the Lisa Sainsbury Foundation will lead the courses, which are being funded by the Joint Advisory Group for Terminal Illness, with moneys from the health authority and the county's social services department. The Volunteer Bureaux were actively involved in the discussions about the courses. (Project No. 17)

(d) Colchester Health Promotion Unit – working with voluntary organisations to help promote better health

Colchester is getting a number of partnerships off the ground: Youth Outreach, a partnership between the Youth Enquiry Service (a voluntary group) and the health promotion unit. The aim is to 'provide an outreach service to help young people deal with "sensitive issues"'; a training project to train CABx staff in issues which surround HIV; and a breast-screening service carried out in conjunction with Colchester Hospital League of Friends. 'We have had lots of co-operation from local media', they report, 'and a great deal of public support'. (Project No. 121)

(e) North Tees Health Promotion Unit – training voluntary counsellors

North Tees Health Promotion Unit is training voluntary counsellors working with drugs, HIV/AIDS and women's health placements. All voluntary counsellors are 'supervised by a professional worker, and there is mutual understanding of voluntary and statutory roles' . . . 'Although some of the volunteers have been unsuitable for certain tasks, this has been overcome by offering them alternative tasks.' (Project No. 131)

(f) Quitline – a voluntary organisation developing training for the corporate sector

Quitline runs a 'Quit in Five' stop-smoking course, which was developed in 1988 for use on company premises. A five-session stop-smoking course, run by trained co-ordinators, it takes smokers through the main steps in stopping smoking. Quit is an independent charity, funded by donations and course fees, and it also receives some funding from the HEA. (Project No. 85)

(g) Lewisham and North Southwark Alcohol Advisory Council – training youth workers to provide information about the sensible use of alcohol

Lewisham and North Southwark Alcohol Advisory Council are running a pilot project, Alcohol and Young People, to offer training courses to youth and project workers. This voluntary organisation (with input from local NHS staff, police and other services) works directly with young people. The aim is to develop knowledge and awareness of alcohol in both its personal and social contexts, and to help them use this knowledge to promote sensible drinking and help reduce the harm caused by drinking problems – social and medical. (Project No. 92)

2. Campaigning and advocacy

(a) Age Well – country-wide initiatives to promote good health among older people – partnerships between health professionals and the voluntary organisation Age Concern England

The numerous Age Well initiatives would take up a book in themselves, and are an astonishing example of partnership.

Older people now make up over 20 per cent of the population. Age Well is a nationwide campaign originally orchestrated in July 1985 by the Health Education Council (as it was then known) in collaboration with Age Concern England, to encourage positive approaches to the promotion of health in later life. It formed part of the Health Education Council's Health in Old Age programme, and the initial two-year campaign stimulated widespread local activity. The campaign 'identified the important role in joint planning between local government, health authorities and voluntary agencies for achieving lasting changes in the health of older people'.[2]

Following the demise of the Health in Old Age programme area in March 1990, Age Concern England has taken over sole responsibility for Age Well (a special six-month hand-over grant being made available up to September 1990). The Age Well programme continues to involve groups like the Centre for Health and Retirement Education and health and social services agencies.

Examples of the range of activities that have formed part of Age Well range from one-off events, such as

- a two-day event on Health in Old Age held in Liverpool in 1989 – with 32 workshops including crime prevention, breast screening, DIY, nutrition and housing
- an 'Age-Well' day held in Norwich in March 1990. There were 'taster' sessions of short mat bowls, badminton, swimming, snooker and keep fit. Discussions and workshops on various aspects of health and well-being were held three times during the day. There was also an exhibition with 18 national and local organisations exhibiting

to large joint ventures:

- Salford – the health authority has a comprehensive programme of health promotion for older people. In two areas of the city, local health and social services staff have joined with voluntary organisations to identify the health concerns of older people in relation to services provided. Work is undertaken in community and day centres, and information is provided through local resources including libraries. Public activity is undertaken, such as health fairs and shows and the setting up of a pensioners' health forum.
- Liverpool – a voluntary agency, Age Concern, has brought together a number of agencies throughout the city, providing a range of leisure, recreational and learning activities. Information about existing facilities is disseminated. Many organisations are involved in planning this initiative, including the health authority, educational bodies, voluntary, church and pensioners'

organisations. The health authority has a variety of initiatives with older people, including a community-based project for the 'younger' elderly. (Project No. 43)

(b) The Vegetarian Society – working with statutory authorities to provide more choice in school meals

School meals organisers are actively involved alongside the Vegetarian Society, which is campaigning for the provision of more vegetarian school meals, with their Choice! (for healthy school meals) initiative. (Project No. 53)

(c) The TACT Project – a campaign to bring about wide changes in neighbourhood environment and to foster good mental health

Three years of funding from the Mental Health Unit of Sunderland District Health Authority for the Good Mental Health (TACT) project have just run out. This project was a partnership between people living in the East End of Sunderland, and professional workers from the Mental Health Services, Social Services and Housing Departments. The group 'developed from concerns expressed to TACT workers which included the housing of former mental patients from other parts of the country in inadequate accommodation in the East End area'.

The group's vision:

> an East End where economic, social and environmental factors allow people to feel in control of their own lives as part of a caring community . . .

> We have already made progress. Significant improvements have been made to the housing stock; cleaning up the riverside area has started; there is co-operative housing and some employment co-ops; a modest extension has begun to be built at the community centre. However, unemployment remains among the highest in the country, many families are dependent on supplementary benefit, much harder-to-let housing remains . . . Within such an area community care is stretched to the limits – so many people need support and comparatively few are left to give it.

To play its part in realising the vision, the Good Mental Health Group established principles: fostering good mental health by supporting preventive strategies in the broadest sense; sharing understanding about the neighbourhood; pursuing a policy of integration, not isolation, and education and training. (Project No. 112)

(d) Worthing Women's Health Information Centre – filling a perceived need, and campaigning to provide more facilities for women in the area

The WWHIC came into existence ten years ago: 'We were told by the DHA to go away and prove a need'. After much pressure, a full well-women clinic is running locally, with the information centre providing pregnancy testing facilities twice a week. (Project No. 40)

3. Access

(a) Tower Hamlets Health Strategy Group – a voluntary organisation working to provide help and support to community members – particularly those from minority ethnic groups

Tower Hamlets Health Strategy Group, a combination of voluntary and statutory workers, supports and extends the work of Environmental Health Officers, particularly in relation to minority ethnic groups. This includes the provision of voluntary bilingual pest control linkworkers, and community education and support on other public health issues – rubbish, damp, and housing problems. The project is also 'developing a support network for specialist Bengali-speaking posts in the health authority'. (Project No. 70)

(b) The 493 Project – supported by a voluntary organisation, the Association for the Prevention of Addiction – to give addicts and anyone using drugs access to health services

The 493 Project in London's Tower Hamlets, with its slogan, 'Injecting drugs? We're here to help you stay healthy', is run by the Association for the Prevention of Addiction, but funded by Tower Hamlets RHA and City and Hackney Health Authority. Services offered: free needle exchange, free condoms and advice on safer sex; primary health care services such as dressings, treatment of abscesses and HIV tests, and social services such as referrals for legal advice, housing, welfare rights, medical care, counselling and support. (Project No. 86)

(c) Home Visiting Link Scheme – a voluntary organisation that recognises cultural differences, and works to give access to minority ethnic groups

The Home Visiting Link Scheme – provided by Worcester Racial Equality Council – provides a service in Worcester to visit ethnic minority families with health or related problems by interpreting/giving advice/assistance in a variety of areas. ESL home tuition is offered to back up the other services. (Project No. 71)

(d) Voluntary agencies working to provide linkworkers to give pregnant minority ethnic women and their babies access to health services

Tyne and Wear Racial Equality Council and Newcastle DHA provide a service to support and advise ethnic minority women through delivery; similarly, Maternity Links, based in Bristol, use linkworkers 'to meet the needs of Asian women in Bristol, and to provide support, understanding, information and interpreting to pregnant non-English speaking women and their children using the health service' (Maternity Links: Project No. 6; Midwifery Project for the Bangladeshi Community: Project No. 10)

(e) Radio Action Trust: broadcasting to the Asian community on health

The Department of Health is backing innovative work to broadcast to the Asian community in the Midlands. The Radio Action Trust is launching a project, Health Matters for All, funded by the Department to publicise health issues to Asian communities in Coventry and Leicester, through two local radio stations. (Project No. 41)

(f) Save the Children Fund – working in partnership with many statutory agencies

Save the Children Fund is involved in a number of innovative partnerships with statutory agencies:

- In Sunderland, Save the Children is working with Sunderland Health Authority, Sunderland Borough Council, the Urban Aid Programme, economic development agencies and local residents to fund and run the Pennywell Neighbourhood Centre – a neighbourhood house from which a variety of health workers and others undertake community and group work initiatives.

  An independent evaluator of the project is also being funded as part of the costs. The group reports that 'there has been considerable support for this multidisciplinary approach. The main problem is ensuring that time committed to the centre is adhered to on the part of agency staff who are operating under the pressures of their usual workload. (Project No. 106)

- In Newcastle, Save the Children is running a number of projects. Going for Growth, is based in several inner-city areas of Newcastle upon Tyne, where children are growing at rates far below their potential, when compared to children from more affluent parts of the city. Save the Children Fund is acting in partnership with the Child Health Department of Newcastle University and several Newcastle communities, to identify the reasons why children fail to grow and to seek ways to help all children in the community reach their full potential. Community involvement is central to the project, and discussions among the Bangladeshi community have already identified lack of support for new mothers and the lack of halal baby food as being reasons why children from that community may not be receiving an adequate diet. (Project No. 109)

- Also in Newcastle, Save the Children is in partnership with Newcastle Health Authority, Newcastle Social Services and local residents, to support the Cowgate Children's Centre. This partnership has been going for two-and-a-half years, and provides a playgroup for 40 children, together with activities for parents, including emphasis on healthy eating and healthy lifestyles. Save the Children notes that 'local people speak well of the centre, and the agencies are looking to extend the partnership'. (Project No. 107.) Cowgate was the subject of an evaluation report, published by Save the Children.

- The Riverside Child Health Project is a third Newcastle programme of outreach work, including the design and contribution of information for minority groups, that has been established for eight years with the help of

Save the Children, in partnership with the health authority and the local authority. Both sides provide substantial funding. The health authority also contributes a team of doctors and speech therapists, and the city council provides funding and a building to house the project. As with other Save the Children projects, the partnership is being independently evaluated. (Project No. 108)

(g) Deptford Family Resource Centre – specialist support for minority ethnic families

Deptford Family Resource Centre provides specialist health support – for Vietnamese and West African women and children, and their families. There is a Vietnamese parent and toddler group, a West African surgery and home visiting by linkworkers. Partners are Save the Children, Guy's Hospital, and local health authorities, who refer families to the centre.

'Identifying specific needs and aiming for a wider understanding of the child in the context of its family and culture', is one objective of the project, which has been going for 18 months, and is evaluated, say Save the Children, on the increased numbers of Vietnamese and West African families using the resource centres. The positive benefits of the project have been more inter-agency links and networking. 'The project is taken seriously by other professionals and users. Language difficulties were initially a problem but employment of linkworkers with Vietnamese and Yoruba as mother tongue overcame this. Building trust was a lengthy process', notes the questionnaire. (Project No. 111)

(h) CLASH (Central London Action on Street Health) – helping those living rough to gain access to better health

CLASH (Central London Action on Street Health) is a partnership formed as a response to growing awareness (in 1985) by a number of statutory and voluntary sector agencies that HIV/AIDS was an important issue for young people in Central London, particularly as many of these young people were 'disenfranchised from the majority of statutory service provision, particularly health services' (CLASH bi-annual report, 1987–89). CLASH aims to liaise between the statutory and voluntary sectors, representing their clients' needs to these services. CLASH is a health education and HIV prevention project devised jointly by representatives from the Bloomsbury District Counselling Service, the Bloomsbury Health Education Department, the Basement Youth Project, the Hungerford Drug Project, the Soho Project, and the Terrence Higgins Trust. It is funded and resourced by Bloomsbury Health authority and various charitable trusts, including the Monument Trust.

The CLASH bi-annual report 1987–89 notes:

> Over the last two years CLASH has grown from a project [comprising] three individuals with a new and untried supervision/management structure into a strong team and an established service . . . This has been due to the CLASH

project workers past and present, and the support of the statutory and voluntary sector representation on the project's steering group ... The experience of working within the project and managing it has been new to all those involved and has on occasions meant challenging established patterns of working. (Project No. 128)

(i) The Chinese Health and Information Centre in Manchester – an example of alternative health provision serving one community

The Chinese Health and Information Centre (CHIC) was set up in 1987 following the initial work of a Chinese GP who held a regular health clinic in a Chinese Sunday School, and is now a professionally-run health centre run by a multi-agency, multi-sectoral steering committee. It aims to give the Chinese community better access to health and to the NHS. All workers are bilingual, and the centre is run by a steering committee, which includes members of the funding statutory services. It provides free services including a branch surgery staffed by Chinese doctors who give advice to clients from all over central Manchester and surrounding areas; a drop-in facility staffed by nurses and workers who speak a range of Chinese dialects and give advice on health topics and the use of the health services; a telephone service for advice and interpreting; health education materials translated into Chinese or adapted from other sources. The centre has produced detailed evaluation of its work (see Appendix 3). (Project No. 14)

4. Self-help

(a) The Manchester Self-help Resource Centre – providing a resource network for self-help groups

There are many flourishing self-help groups throughout Manchester, and support is offered to these groups by a variety of organisations. However, says the centre, 'support offered is fragmented and is usually only a small part of each agency's wider work. The Self-help Resource Centre is the only resource and information agency which works in depth with self-help groups'. Originally funded by Opportunities for Volunteering, it is now funded by Joint Finance.

The project was originally established in 1986 and aims

- to build on existing services which serve self-help groups so that the support on offer is more easily accessible and better co-ordinated
- to work with statutory and voluntary agencies to provide the liaison, back-up support and training functions which self-help groups require
- to promote the concept of issues involved in self-help, and to facilitate understanding and confidence among embryonic and existing self-help groups
- to network self-help groups and encourage mutual support and sharing between them
- to develop joint initiatives with professionals and service providers in

promoting the concept of self-help and to increase understanding and confidence in working with self-help groups

- to provide information about and to groups through outreach work and telephone/written contact. (Project No. 115)

(b) Walsall Mastectomy and Breast Cancer Self-help Group – many partnerships are developing with voluntary organisations providing ancillary support and sympathy for patients undergoing a surgical trauma – a softer edge that they believe is not offered by the NHS

The group states:

> Our self-help group was founded in 1983 by local mastectomees, to provide emotional support (not available from the NHS) for all ladies who face the trauma presented by diagnosis and treatment of breast cancer. We do NOT see counselling as giving specific medical advice or information, not making judgements but rather as a means of using our personal experiences and skills to help others talk through and sort out a problem. (Project No. 19)

(c) The Restricted Growth Association – working in partnership with the hospital

The association, in conjunction with Sheffield University, have for the past two years run a counselling service for families and patients attending the limb-lengthening clinic at Sheffield Children's Hospital. The service provided is complementary to the surgical care offered by the hospital with parental support being offered from first appointment at Outpatients. Counselling is both on an individual and group discussion basis, to explore patients' 'hopes and fears in undergoing this surgical procedure'. (Project No. 7)

(d) Northampton's 'Dialabetic' Service – self-help support for diabetics

Northampton's 'Dialabetic' Service runs a telephone counselling helpline for people with diabetes. The Northampton Branch of the BDA funds and runs the service, and the consultant physician at the local general hospital provides training and referrals to the service. (Project No. 59)

5. Information and education

(a) Cancer Support Groups – an area where many voluntary organisations are working within the NHS to provide further education and information for patients

The Worcester Cancer Support Group provides an information stand in the oncology department of the local hospital, and Tunbridge Wells Cancer Help Centre sends 'helpers/counsellors to patients in Pembury Hospital who are undergoing radiotherapy. 'This has been at the request of the nurses, who are very keen on what we have to offer', they say. (Worcester Cancer Support Group: Project No. 26; Tunbridge Wells Cancer Help Centre: Project No. 21)

(b) Nottingham Help Directory – a directory of help and information for the locality

Produced as a result of co-operation between Nottingham Council for Voluntary Service, Social Services, Library Services and the Health Authority, which combined resources to produce an annual directory of helping agencies within the area of the health authority. (Project 61)

(c) Rushcliffe CVS – providing health information to fit in with working women's needs

Rushcliffe Council for Voluntary Service – whose Women's Health and Diet Group 10-week course was designed to run in the lunch-hour to address the needs of women who are working and could not use the courses offered at local adult education classes.

They say, in a note on development work, that they were helped by 'a variety of professional colleagues, including health visitors, a dietitian, librarian, alternative therapist, and the administrator from the breast screening unit. There were useful sessions, and on the basis of charging £1 per session, the CVS made a profit of almost £100 which was then fed into voluntary action in the borough.' (Project No. 95)

(d) A national support network for health information that supports health information in the media in a way ideal for today's lifestyle

Broadcasting Support Services – is a charity whose helplines (particularly the National AIDS Helpline) reach out into the community. They run a 40-line phone system in London, Manchester and Cardiff, on topics ranging across the fields of health, social welfare, education, the environment and recreation. They provide administrative services to TV appeals, and also provide a bolt-on service to supplement DoH advice – part funding comes from the Department of Health in exchange for an agreement for the service to answer calls for advice from readers of the Department's door-to-door leaflets. Qualitative evaluation of the helpline showed that people found it was 'immediate, non-threatening, confidential, anonymous, convenient, personal and easy to use and re-use'. (Project No. 91)

(e) The Health Store – voluntary organisations providing confidential information to young people

The Health Store is a new project which is a partnership between North Warwickshire Health Promotion Service and Talking Shop, a voluntary group providing confidential counselling for young people. (Project No. 129)

(f) Harrogate and Area Council for Voluntary Service – forming a team with the statutory services to produce dedicated information material on cancer

In order to extend what could be provided by the health service, the Macmillan Nursing Service approached Harrogate and Area Council for Voluntary Service to produce a leaflet giving information, advice, support, practical help and fundraising for people with cancer. As Harrogate and Area Council for Voluntary Service put it:

> Our first meeting was in June 1989. Eighteen representatives of voluntary organisations, together with delegates from Social Services, the Health Service and the Community Health Council attended . . . A sub-group put together the information and met regularly to report back. At the same time we learned about an excellent booklet that had been produced by the Cancer Relief Macmillan Fund in October 1989, showing national contacts for people with cancer. We obtained permission to use their booklet alongside our own.
>
> The Health Promotion Unit of the Harrogate Health Authority has assisted with the editing and printing of the leaflet. It was distributed in May 1990 throughout the Harrogate District together with the Macmillan booklet, to all doctors' practices and hospitals as well as outlets such as CHC and the CABx. (Project No. 127)

(g) The Meningitis Trust – utilising suppport from health professionals to get their message across

The Trust says

> We have encountered great willingness on behalf of two medical advisers from the health authority to listen to and take account of the views of the lay people at the Trust.
>
> Some of our voluntary local support groups have also developed very successful partnerships with the health professionals in their area. The most outstanding example is our Merseyside Group, who have worked closely with the Consultant in Public Health Medicine, Dr John Reid. Dr Reid has promoted and distributed the Trust's literature within the health authority, done joint statements to the press with the group members, and keeps them informed of cases of meningitis in the area. He also makes sure that families who have been affected by meningitis are aware of the group, and of the help they can offer. For their part, the group provide the Trust's information, give talks to medical staff and lay groups about meningitis, and act as an independent voice to support the health authority. (Project No. 83)

(h) The Breakthrough Trust – 'Have you Heard?': a Directory of Birmingham's Resources and Information for Hearing-Impaired People (1989)

The Breakthrough Trust Deaf–Hearing Integration is a charity which encourages integration between deaf and hearing children and adults by bringing them into continuous contact with each other through a variety of social activities and practical projects. The Centre, based in Birmingham, runs total communications courses and workshops for mixed groups of professionals and lay people who wish to communicate with a deaf person; telecommunications information and training; parent and toddler family drop-in contact group; children's book and toy library; holiday projects; library and information resources service. Funded by five Birmingham health authorities, in 1989 it produced a guide to resources for hearing-impaired people in the area. (Project No. 50)

(i) TACADE – Skills for the Primary School Child Project

TACADE (the Advisory Council on Alcohol and Drug Education) and Re-Solv have joined together to produce a skills-based child protection programme for primary schools. The programme aims to promote a partnership between school, home and people in the community who work in school in helping children to make healthy and safe choices. The resource includes material for school staff, community workers and governors, parents and people at home and children aged from 5 to 11 years.

The funding for the project has come from a number of sources of which the Department of Education and Science has been a major contributor. (Project No. 13)

6. Policy development

(a) Living Options – voluntary organisations helping disabled people to have full involvement in their care

Living Options is a national programme sponsored by the King's Fund, which aims to bring particular groups into the planning process. Northallerton and District CHC were keen to take part. One of the strategies of the project is to involve users:

> central to Living Options in practice is the commitment to the full participation of disabled people (and their advocates) in planning, designing, implementing and monitoring the services they use. Strategies for consulting people with disabilities, including those who are less articulate or able, need to be developed; issues about representation must be addressed; and structures for the ongoing participation of consumers in service provision must be evolved. (Project No. 103)

(b) Lewisham and North Southwark Alcohol Advisory Council – voluntary organisations helping to devise policy for the corporate sector

Alcohol workplace policies – where organisations like Lewisham and North Southwark Alcohol Advisory Committee offer advice and assistance to employers in the development and implementation of workplace alcohol policies. (Project No. 92)

(c) Joint Planning in Southampton – an example of voluntary organisation involvement in strategic planning of health services

Southampton and South West Hants Health District have set up a number of joint planning groups (JPGs) with representatives from various agencies:

> Health, Social Services, Education, Environmental Health, FPC, Health Education, City Health Education, Health for All Co-ordinators and the voluntary sector are all represented. The representation of the voluntary sector has been called 'Making it Happen' and representatives get together occasionally to report on the work of our own JPGs. Representatives of the different agencies have been supportive to each other, and the full JPG has at times been a mighty influence in encouraging less enthusiastic agencies to respond to their own representatives. (Project No. 140)

(d) Newham Alcohol Advisory Service

NAAS is a voluntary agency that receives its core funding from the local authority, the District Health Authority and from the Department of Health. There is also support from the Mental Health Foundation, the King's Fund and from trusts. NAAS offers counselling and advice to people with alcohol-related problems, and their families, and works towards the prevention of alcohol problems by increasing public awareness of the effects of alcohol, and by challenging attitudes through education and training. NAAS worked with both the health authority and the local authority to develop a district policy document on alcohol in the workplace, and a copy of the policy was given to every member of the staff of both authorities when it was launched in 1989. (Project No. 47)

7. Service provision

The following are all examples of voluntary organisations which are working in partnership with the statutory services to deliver better services and to provide better care for patients. In many such cases, voluntary organisations have secured premises and services that would not have been achieved otherwise.

(a) The Neuro-Care Team

One example of a new partnership (begun in March 1990) is the Neuro-Care Team, a collaborative exercise between national and local voluntary organisations (the Parkinson's Disease Society, Multiple Sclerosis Society, MNDA, Friedrich's Ataxia and Dystonia Societies, and the Barking, Havering and Brentwood District Health Authority. The Neuro-Care Team is based at Harold Wood Hospital in Essex, and works with newly-diagnosed patients in Dr Leslie Findlay's clinics and wards. The pilot project aims 'to provide an enhanced standard of care for people who are newly-diagnosed for the above conditions, and to offer a patient-centred approach. Its main features are:

- a multi-disciplinary team which straddles the hospital–community divide and in which any member can suggest initiatives
- recognition of patients' needs for information (adapted to their own situation) at all stages of their illness but especially around the time of diagnosis
- special attention to the patient as a 'whole person' and to the social and emotional aspects of long-term illness
- the involvement of patients and carers in monitoring and decision-making. (Project No. 126)

(b) National Schizophrenia Fellowship

The partnership between East Birmingham District Health Authority and the National Schizophrenia Fellowship provides a multi-purpose day, evening and weekend service for schizophrenia sufferers. The Fellowship – funded by the DHA – provides an employment project (Footprint, which includes work placements within East Birmingham Hospital), the development of a housing consortium and a drop-in club.

The partnership has been going for two years and is evaluated by the local Care Planning Team. Positive benefits have been 'changed attitudes in Health/Social Services relationships', says the National Schizophrenia Fellowship, 'though we do find a great deal of red tape within the statutory services which makes us, the voluntary organisation, the lead agency'. (Project No. 114)

(c) Devon and Cornwall Autistic Society

The partnership between the regional and District Health Authorities and Devon and Cornwall Autistic Society, who with the Devon and Cornwall Autistic Community Trust provide residential care and training for sixteen profoundly handicapped autistic adults. They also run a day centre. The NHS bodies have representation on the management committee and provide specific nursing expertise and staff training. The local authority is also involved in the partnership – contributing money to cover fees, together with support and advice. All the partners are represented on the management committee. (Project No. 54)

(d) The Eastwood Tuesday Club – Nottingham

The club was set up by Eastwood Volunteer Bureau and community psychiatric nurses, two-and-a-half years ago. It is so successful that another club has been started on a Thursday. Volunteers, in partnership with community psychiatric nurses for the elderly provided by Nottingham Health Authority, set out to 'provide an enjoyable time out for senile dementia sufferers and a break for their carers in this rural area'. (Project No. 104)

(e) The Food Chain – London

The Food Chain – a London-wide volunteer service that delivers healthy, nutritious meals to people with HIV–related illnesses. Patients are referred by a third party – usually Social Services, hospital, or AIDS charity. With advice from hospital dietitians, and the help of the volunteers, the Food Chain cooks a weekly Sunday lunch. The service began in 1989 by delivering meals to 25 home-bound people, now – through voluntary organisations, NHS and local authority referrals – the numbers are up to 120. Funding from the service comes via 'pay-backs' from Social Services departments across London.

Forty volunteer drivers deliver the meals, anonymously, on a rota basis. Meals are nutritious, appetising, and non-standard – they try to follow the likes and dislikes of the client, and provide ethnic and vegetarian meals, for both patient, families and carers.

The organiser collaborated with a local church and in essence, the project is a partnership between the church, which provides the community centre where the cooking is done; volunteers who provide the backbone of the service, and voluntary organisations, NHS and local authorities who both refer patients to it, and contribute towards costs.

WHAT MAKES FOR SUCCESS IN PARTNERSHIP?

Throughout our cases studies we encountered common threads both inside and outside the partnership that made it work. Inside the partnership, the following were key criteria for success:

- openness and honesty
  about the possibilities and limitations of the partnership and what it is setting out to achieve – sharing the same vision and understanding each other's problems. Objectives and obligations should be set out in advance, and agreement on how the project will be monitored and evaluated should be reached at the outset and built in to the project.

> 'Not being able to communicate with officials when you have a voice is bad enough, but it's dreadful when you are miming and they either can't lip read or just won't try.' (secretary of laryngectomy support group)

- mutual respect
  partnerships where one side has a 'hidden agenda' simply won't work.
  A balance of skills is needed – and although these may not seem the same, they should have equal weight within the partnership. One side may be bringing 'professional' skills, the other 'lay' skills, but each is just as valid.
  Being friends (either through working together on a previous project, or through long acquaintance) brings an added dimension to the partnership.

Lay staff also need to be able to hold and win respect from health professionals involved. The latter will need to be committed to the principles of the project, and to the idea of working with a voluntary organisation.

- flexible, dynamic leadership
within each of the partnership teams – entirely committed to making it work, to solving problems and to looking for opportunities for the partnership to progress.

> 'All money for office expenses, and help for members and their families has to be raised locally, and although we have been established for over six years we find the medical and nursing professions do not co-operate in any way. When approached professionally, they either say they do not know of us or murmur "they do great work", and leave it at that. We hear increasingly from people diagnosed as cancer patients who feel absolutely shattered by the news and need information and counselling but have not been advised by the medical profession that this can be obtained from us.' (cancer support group)

There are also outside factors which create a good climate for partnership:

- *secure funding* has to be the prime consideration. A working party established by NCVO reported that: '. . . to ensure careful forward planning and budgeting, any effective organisation needs a reasonable core of predictable income. Without such core funding, enthusiasm, expertise and energy can be dissipated.'[3]

  Given the trend by many funders to look for short-term project-related funding, health promotion partnerships need a secure base on which to operate and to look for other funds. Ideally, Section 64 funding would provide the mechanism for this, although such funding is based on a three-year allocation, reviewed annually on performance, and can be withdrawn at any time. The threat of withdrawal hanging over a project is clearly not ideal for partnership to thrive, and can create a situation where staff are looking for 'safe' options in terms of the work they do, rather than innovative ideas.

  Many projects were uncertain as to where to obtain advice on funding, and on how to put in a proposal. There is also the fear of being compromised by accepting funding – the compromise being agreement to refrain from addressing certain issues, or not working in conflict with other bodies.

- *providing a reasonable 'base'*: like any small business venture, a partnership needs its own form of identity: reasonable premises, office and computer equipment. Some partnerships have been able to use premises belonging to the statutory services, others have not been so lucky. The effect of working in a reasonable environment cannot be overstated – professional premises and equipment will allow a project to achieve a professional standard of work.

- *flexible funding for support staffing* – with the 'headspace' to grow if the project develops. Many projects are restricted in terms of the staff they can recruit, simply because they are on short-term project-related moneys. For example, this may mean that only temporary secretarial staff can be recruited – expensive in cost, and with no guarantee of sharing the rest of the team's aims and objectives.

- *providing training in other skills* – sometimes thought to be 'fringe' but which are vital – e.g. book-keeping, project management, evaluation.

   Many staff members in voluntary organisations are placed in a position of responsibility without adequate training. Some volunteer members may never have worked in an office.

- *senior staff who 'champion' the project*: usually within the health service, these 'mentors' can secure funding, open channels of communication, legitimise ways of working. Also important is other day-to-day support within the local health service hierarchy.

- *patience and encouragement* to be free to work outside the usual constraints: 'time in lieu', flexible interpretation of job descriptions.

- *creating a climate* that encourages risk-taking and innovation and does not punish failure.

'What is important for the statutory sector is:

(a) Not assuming you can do it alone

(b) Listening to, discussing with, and being accessible

(c) Being open in public about plans and decisions

(d) Taking chances, and backing the outsider if you feel they are the right agency

(e) Being flexible and above all imaginative about how your 'might' can help agencies deliver

(f) Being clear and open about the holes, the reasons for them, and acknowledging their existence

(g) Accepting that you will never be able to get it 'right' for everyone but still trying to do so

(h) Knowing you will always be the kicking post, because of the 'gaps', which will always be there.'

THE PITFALLS OF PARTNERSHIP

What are the 'rocks' that partnerships need to steer clear of?

Conflicts of interest

It has to be acknowledged that there can be conflicts of interest over the question of accountability – or, just who is the 'client' – the NHS or the community?

   One of the projects reported 'We believe there is a difference in philosophy regarding confidentiality between the statutory sector and the voluntary sector – in our project, discussion on this is still taking place'.

Ask (Project No. 133) is a youth counselling and information service being run in Lincoln – a Lincoln CVS project. It provides a free and confidential counselling, information and pregnancy testing services for young people (aged 12–25) in Lincoln and the surrounding area. The partners are North Lincolnshire Health Authority, which provides a 'qualified nurse, midwife, health visitor' (one person!) who is seconded to the scheme to carry out pregnancy testing and to give advice. She comes under Ask's rules of confidentiality and procedures when dealing with clients. The service is used by young people who are afraid or unwilling to use their GP or a health centre. 'It is', say Ask, 'gaining a reputation as a confidential and professional service for young people. We keep records – not personal details – enquiries, tests and subsequent action, and the health authority are considering expanding the service to offer a full sexual matters and contraception clinic for young people with additional seconded staff and training for volunteers.'[4]

Some partnerships have already addressed the question:

> Salford Community Health Project workers have negotiated a clause in their job description which acknowledges this issue: 'The prime responsibility of community workers is to the community they serve rather than to the agency which employs them. The Health Authority undertakes to respect that, in accordance with the analogy of clinical freedom awarded to professional staff. The Authority also undertakes that it cannot expect the worker to act as its agent in any conflict with the community served.'[5]

This 'fiercely partisan' approach may not be a barrier – but it does need to be addressed in any question of joint working.

The following were also criteria for failure:

- loss of funding: many partnerships exist on short-term funding linked to specific projects. Many have to pay out their own costs in advance and wait for funding to arrive. It is unreasonable to expect a partnership to act in a business-like and productive way when denied the secure funding it needs to survive.
- loss of key staff: enthusiastic staff are often a key reason why a project achieves many things and attracts support from its clients.
- changing political agendas which remove the hierarchical support from the project, 'starving it out' through lack of information, lack of time, lack of access to networks and other support.
- lack of delegation – for example, lack of clear boundaries within the management structure can mean that members who are intended to have a 'steering' role become involved in the day-to-day management of the project.
- conflicts of ownership or the problems of 'careerism' – not letting pride/ ambition stand in the way of making a successful project. One partner may find it difficult to 'stand back' to allow the other to win praise for what will be seen as an achievement.
- the imposition of unreal expectations on the partnership which cannot be met.
- unrealistic time-frames. As stated in a review of the achievements of one community health project: 'In a time-limited project of three years, there is

pressure to produce visible results quickly, and there is not enough time for realistic or appropriate evaluation; this does not do justice to the community or the community development approach.'[5]

- partnerships growing in such a way that they lose touch with the original 'customers' they serve – the need to ensure that the committees do not become too remote from the users. 'Small-time but long-term' members retain their value.

NOTES AND REFERENCES

1   *Link Up* newsletter, Walsall Mastectomy and Breast Cancer Support Group.
2   *Age Well Case Studies*, Age Concern.
3   *Effectiveness and the Voluntary Sector*, report of a working party established by NCVO. NCVO, 1990.
4   Ask questionnaire, Project No. 133.
5   Policy quoted in Rosemary Cox and Gail Findlay, *Cambridge Health Authority Community Development Health Project: a Review of Achievements So Far*. Health Promotion Service, Cambridge, 1990.

5 NEW OPPORTUNITIES

WHAT OPPORTUNITIES FOR PARTNERSHIP WILL CHANGES IN THE NHS BRING?

The changing shape of the NHS and the redefining of roles within it are creating many new opportunities for partnership with voluntary organisations.

1. RHAs: There will be more autonomy for Regional Health Authorities to act creatively, using local resources. Voluntary organisations should seek to ensure wherever possible that working in partnership with the voluntary sector is included as part of the Regional Health Authority's strategic planning.

2. DHAs: District Health Authorities will be increasingly more flexible, and may be looking to purchase health promotion initiatives from a variety of sources – which could include the voluntary sector, providing the service offered is both sufficiently high quality, and is cost-effective. DHAs will increasingly be looking to develop contractual relationships with voluntary organisations, where the obligations of the relationship are clearly defined.

3. GPs and FHSAs:
    These two 'new players' now have a vested interest in providing health promotion. Again, they will be open to creating a dialogue with voluntary organisations, and could increasingly look to the voluntary sector to offer a broad range of health promotion initiatives.

    Individual FHSAs will, for the first time, employ 'independent medical advisers' (IMAs) to provide them with an independent source of medical advice, and to help define standards. The IMA will be particularly involved in questions of indicative prescribing and audit, and will visit all GP practices in each area. FHSAs have a real opportunity to use the IMAs as a conduit to feed out information on work with voluntary organisations in the area, and to encourage new initiatives involving voluntary organisations.

4. Health promotion units:
    Health promotion units may almost become 'trading agencies' in their own right, and will have a dual role to play both as contract specifiers and as agents for service delivery. They will increasingly be looking to work with voluntary organisations which can provide high quality skills.

THE CONTRACT CULTURE

The influence of the 'contract culture' is being felt in all areas which involve voluntary organisations – it could be the most important challenge of all to voluntary organisations.

Changes in the structure of the NHS are sweeping in a climate of contracting: parts of the Health Service are having to become used to buying and selling to and from each other. Contracting needs to ensure that the best quality of service for the eventual consumer will be provided, and that the parties to the contract have a clear understanding of what their joint relationship entails.

In 1989 NCVO convened a working group on contracting out and, as part of this work, has published a series of guidance notes on this subject. The group laid down a series of basic principles which they believe should guide voluntary organisations interested in becoming involved in contracting.

6 *RECOMMENDATIONS*

In a very short period of time, this report has identified over 140 partnerships in health promotion between voluntary organisations and parts of the NHS. Examples considered to represent 'good practice' in collaboration between the voluntary and statutory sectors have been singled out.

The way forward

Some partnerships have all the right ingredients to thrive – they have support, keen workers, a professional and committed approach, but lack the vital spark. This could be secure funding, or a clear channel that will help them take steps to remind those parts of the NHS around them that they are a potential partner. The following recommendations will help partnerships between the two sectors to increase in number and to become better established.

RECOMMENDATIONS

(a) **Planning**

The group recommends that government take on board the role and potential for voluntary organisations in both the planning of health services, and the setting of targets to be achieved in health promotion.

The group further suggests that in order to achieve this, specific references to work with the voluntary sector be included in Regional Health Planning Reviews, which are now carried out annually by the Department of Health with each Regional Health Authority.

The group also suggests that FHSAs should include specific suggestions to GPs to encourage working with the voluntary sector, through whatever means they consider appropriate, including the independent medical adviser employed by each FHSA.

(b) **Funding**

Secure, long-term funding is the key issue to most partnerships, many of which currently do not receive Section 64 or other core funding, and are therefore often attempting to make long-term plans on a patchwork foundation of project-by-project funding from a variety of sources.

The group therefore proposes that consideration be given to the setting up of a special fund (outside existing funds such as Section 64, or Opportunities for Volunteering). This fund – 'a partnerships fund' – would be dedicated to funding voluntary organisations that proposed to carry out health promotion in collaboration with a statutory partner. The group proposes that partnerships applying for funding be asked to fulfil the following criteria:

- that the work of the partnership would be based upon the principles of 'Health for All' described in this report (pp. 9–11)
- that the partnership would operate an equal opportunities policy
- that the partnership was committed to developing the highest quality of health promotion service, and would aim to contract their service into the NHS
- that the partnership recognises the importance of developing evaluation mechanisms, and would build these in from the outset of each piece of work. The group would like to see specific help given by an agency such as the Health Education Authority, perhaps by the 'pairing' of each group with a professional evaluator. Funding should be included to cover this.

Funding should also be provided to cover:

- effective training of staff (particularly for short-term/voluntary staff).

(c) Sharing and dissemination of information

There is a need for:

- co-ordination of activities on health promotion involving the voluntary sector
- an effective networking system to allow those active in the field to learn from each other's activities through reports on replicable projects and general information exchange
- a recognised information resource regarding the benefits of health promotion in areas which are not included in the HEA's Strategic Plan.

The group would like to see the creation of a specific point of contact to address all the above points, and recommends that appropriate funding be provided for the establishment of an arrangement (perhaps in the form of a post or posts based at the HEA) which would allow NCVO and the HEA, jointly, to create such a network.

Other recommendations:

- the group recommends that people in the field should be encouraged to 'cross the divide' between statutory and voluntary sector in order to create better understanding of each other's abilities and therefore greater potential in partnership. This may rest on generosity of funding arrangements, to make it possible for relevant people in partnerships to spend time with 'opposite numbers' in other organisations
- the group would like to see encouragement given to the involvement of the target group themselves in the planning and implementation of health

promotion partnerships (for example, Age Concern England would like to see the involvement of older people themselves in the planning of health promotion ventures related to older people).

(d) Follow-up to this report

The group suggests that the recommendations of this report be reviewed by the HEA/NCVO in one year's time.

Appendix 1 THE PROJECT ADVISORY GROUP

Members of the Project Advisory Group who have attended at least one meeting of the project.

Kay Young* *NCVO*
Amanda Jordan* *NCVO*
Janet Hunter* *NCVO*
Mike Bieber* *Cancerlink*
Dianne Hayter* *Alcohol Concern*
Christine Gowdridge* *Maternity Alliance*
Robin Moss * *Independent Broadcasting Authority*
Noel Baker *Sickle Cell Society*
Zoe Heritage* *HEA Primary Care Unit, Oxford*
Loraine Ashton *Health Education Authority*
Derek Day *National Association of Health Authorities and Trusts*
Elizabeth Anionwu *Sickle Cell Society*
Tony Chiva *Centre for Health and Retirement Education*
Gerry Tibbs* *Health Education Authority*
Richard Paulson *Association of Community Health Councils for England and Wales (ASCHCE&W)*
Hilary Pearce *Age Concern England*
Kim Dueck *Age Concern England*
Ros Meek *Health Visitors' Association*
Jamie Taylor *Terrence Higgins Trust*
Jane Lethbridge* *National Community Health Resource*
Valcric Gillespie *Action with Communities in Rural England (ACRE)*
Dr Joan Lennard *Royal College of GPs*
Jeff French *Society of Health Education and Health Promotion Officers*
Peter Anderson *HEA Primary Care Unit, Oxford*
Dr Harvey Gordon *Association of County Councils*
Renée Myers *Society of FPCs/FHSAs*
Ray Cross (observer) *Department of Health*
Graham Cooke (observer) *Department of Health*

*Member of ad hoc group

Other advisers who have provided information for the project:

Hazel Slavin *South Bank Polytechnic*
Marie Arniitage *UK Health for All Network*

Appendix 2 CASE STUDIES OF PARTNERSHIPS BETWEEN THE STATUTORY AND VOLUNTARY SECTORS

Fifteen projects are included as detailed case studies in this appendix – all were visited in person. As visits progressed and information was submitted, it became clear that these projects had a number of factors in common.

The mentor

First – and in some ways most important of all – each had been launched, and often continued to grow, because of the influence of a 'mentor' figure, usually within the Health Service. This mentor was always at a senior level – two were at Ministerial level, others were Directors of Public Health.

These figures served many purposes. Not least, they helped in the fight for funding from health authority or local authority budgets. They legitimised the projects they represented, cleared pathways through internal bureaucracy and ensured that staff lower down in the management team would give time and support to the project. Their interest in the project guaranteed that even sceptical staff would not obstruct it. The key message for voluntary organisations is to go as high as possible when seeking support for a partnership.

Flexible, dynamic leadership

If support within the statutory authorities is a priority, then leadership within the project is as well. Flexible, dynamic leadership was evident in them all – staff that adopted a positive, 'can do' approach to problems, who would seek opportunities and look for innovative ways in which to work. This sort of project leadership is a two-edged sword for the voluntary sector. Many projects are successful only as long as their key staff remain – one example included in this report – Cambridge Community Development Project – shows that projects founder when lead staff leave, and the project then has to go through a period of 'recuperation'.

Skills and credibility

Skills and credibility with other professionals is vital to voluntary organisations dealing with health professionals. Voluntary organisations need to ensure they are seen to offer a professional service, with skilled staff who are able to deal with health professional queries. One of the case studies – the

Joint Breastfeeding Initiative – recognised that the co-operation of midwifery staff was essential for success, and recruited a very senior midwife into their team.

This may have implications for funding for health promotion projects – will they need to increase their funding to ensure that they can attract health professionals? How vital is it to ensure that voluntary agencies involved in health promotion are seen as having staff of the right calibre?

Mutual respect and understanding

What makes a partnership work? In many cases it is because the parties share the same vision and the same objectives. They understand each other's needs, and respect them, and there is little or no competition between the parties, but a very strong joint effort towards making the project a success. Our chosen collaborations all demonstrated mutual respect between the statutory and the voluntary sector partners, which in some cases had turned into strong and lasting friendship.

A businesslike approach

A businesslike approach is an integral part of success. Administrative functions need to run smoothly, applications for funding need to be properly presented; considerable effort and expense may often need to be put into creating a business-like approach. Again, this brings implications for funding; it is often better to provide skills to organisations and help them grow, rather than impose tasks on them that they cannot meet. Computer equipment, fax machines are essential communication tools of the 1990s, and moneys spent on hiring specialist skills, such as help with fund-raising, computer training, accountancy or public relations, can often ensure that the partnership is given additional strength to develop.

Evaluation

The question of whether and how partnerships should evaluate their work is covered in more detail in Appendix 3. The case studies have all attempted some form of evaluation; from basic counting of clients to, in some cases, very sophisticated analysis by university or other professional evaluators.

Funding

Finally, there is the question of funding. Most of the case studies had been successful in securing continuing funding, but at least one example (Glyndon) went from the brink of disaster in 1990 to expansion in 1991. Secure long-term funding is life or death to partnerships, and the creation of a special fund to allow the development of more partnerships in health promotion is one of the key recommendations made in this report.

THE EIGHT
CATEGORIES OF
PARTNERSHIP

Out of the 143 partnerships contacted, the following are particularly good examples of partnership between the statutory and voluntary sectors. Some have already been included in the text. Others are included in more detail in this appendix.

Specific initiatives

- Joint Breastfeeding Initiative
- Newham Alcohol Advisory Service (p. 53)
- The National Drink-Driving Campaign
- Cancercare, Lancaster
- Breakthrough Trust (p. 51)

Partnerships aiming to provide access

- Chinese Health and Information Centre, Manchester (p. 48)
- Brent Sickle Cell and Thalassaemia Centre
- West Yorkshire Travellers Project

Healthy cities

- The UK Health for All Network
- Hull Healthy City Initiative

Partnerships adopting a community approach

- Bolsover Mental Health Roadshow
- Parkside Health Promotion Unit (p. 23)
- Glyndon Health Project
- Cambridge Community Development Health Project
- Albany Health Project
- Health First – local network (p. 33)

Partnerships giving help and advice

- WHERE (a rural perspective)
- Manchester Self-help Resource Centre (p. 48)
- Preston Health Promotion Unit Media Project with Red Rose Radio

Partnerships with emphasis on providing new NHS facilities

- Mike Heaffey Sports and Rehabilitation Centre

Partnerships creating healthy lifestyles

- The National Forum for Coronary Heart Disease Prevention – School Meals Assessment Project

- TACADE – Skills for the Primary School Child Project (p. 52)

Partnerships empowering the voluntary sector

- Leicester Health Promotion Unit (p. 36)

SPECIFIC INITIATIVES

Joint Breastfeeding Initiative

'Many voluntary organisations are used by health professionals as a means of pushing out their message to the community. We're turning this on its head and using health professionals to push out *our* message – Barbara Henry, Chair, Joint Breastfeeding Initiative

The partners

The voluntary sector: the Breastfeeding Promotion Group of the National Childbirth Trust, La Leche League, and the Association of Breastfeeding Mothers

The statutory sector: Department of Health – health professionals within RHAs, DHAs, hospitals and primary care team (including organisations such as the Health Visitors' Association and the Royal College of Midwives)

History

The JBI was originally proposed by the voluntary sector groups above largely in response to the findings of the 1985 OPCS survey (published in 1988). This indicated that the return to breastfeeding tracked in the 1980 OPCS survey (it had been rising throughout the end of the 1970s) was a 'blip' that had reached a plateau and was possibly about to decline.

In 1990, it is estimated that while 64 per cent of babies born in the UK are routinely breastfed, by the time they are 6 weeks old, only 39 per cent continue to be fed in this way. With breastfeeding being felt by health professionals and medical advice to be the 'best' form of food for babies, both voluntary sector organisations and the Department of Health felt it was time to redress the balance. A campaign was created to target the 'gap' called 'the lost 25 per cent'. The JBI set out to improve the knowledge and practice of breastfeeding management to

- enable those women who choose to breastfeed to continue to do so as long as they wish to
- enable breastfeeding to be seen as a viable option.

Discussions at a WHO meeting in 1988 had led to the Health Visitors' Association and the National Childbirth Trust deciding to convene a

European symposium on breastfeeding and to continue drawing up a Europe-wide strategy for breastfeeding. In the early stages of preparing for this symposium, it became clear that there was no UK-wide strategy and that the plans from the European meeting should be set aside until 'our own house was put in order', says Barbara Henry. From this original idea, three voluntary groups came together to take action: the Breastfeeding Promotion Group of the National Childbirth Trust; La Leche League; and the Association of Breastfeeding Mothers.

Despite the apparent similarity there is little overlap between the three voluntary groups – all three have genuinely different aims and membership, and were (and still are) funded as separate bodies by the Department of Health (Section 64 funding). However, it was agreed by all sides that all three should work together on something that was clearly a joint aim, and in October 1988 the Joint Breastfeeding Initiative was launched.

The chief attraction of the Joint Breastfeeding Initiative is the multi-disciplinary approach. The steering group has members from the voluntary and professional organisations. This balance is reflected in the membership of local groups, and the reason for inviting all the professionals who have contact with the breastfeeding mother is to combat the possibility of 'conflicting advice' from one group to another.

Secure funding

The project exists on short-term (Section 64) funding – but is in the awkward position of trying to make long-term decisions. 'Ideally', says the co-ordinator, Barbara Henry, 'we would be a time-limited project, but we know that it is going to take a significant time to change the status quo.' This creates practical problems in recruiting top-calibre staff that are only solved by the dedication of the voluntary sector – how many chief executives, for example, would switch jobs to one that was only funded for one year at a time?

'One of my fears is that we are expected to operate in a business-like way without business-like funding,' says Barbara.

Mutual respect

A partnership of mutual respect and understanding has developed between the JBI and the Department of Health over the last two years, a fact confirmed by both sides. Each, however, has an awareness about how 'close' they can get to each other, and of the stresses and strains that the relationship imposes.

'Despite the extraordinarily good relationship we have with the Department of Health,' says Barbara Henry, 'there is still the slight feeling on our part of "we'd better keep our noses clean just in case".'

'Voluntary bodies do not always see the Department of Health as their "knight in shining armour", but mandarins will say that they have to answer to Ministers for the money they spend, and equally to be able to say that they have an "effective and cost-effective" method of health promotion in supporting a voluntary body.

'With Section 64 funding being based on the need to foster and keep good relationships, and the need for the Department to justify to Ministers the success of projects, one wonders just how many other voluntary groups suffer from the same fears – and how much this "fear of failure" hampers performance.

'Great warmth exists in the relationship between the key statutory and voluntary partners, and despite the DoH policy of "observer status" which is to inform but not be involved, there is a very great understanding and mutual respect. Only women can breastfeed, so by its very nature it is a feminine issue. And it is fairly natural that it should be spearheaded on both sides by women. However, we believe that the personalities on the project are more important than the fact that it is women working together.'

The mentor

Successful breast-feeding promotion needs the wholehearted support of health professionals, so a mentor was felt to be important to this project on several levels. First of all, Department of Health support was needed for a national campaign to get off the ground. An advocate among the civil servants at the Department was found, and the other bonus – not least in media terms – was that the initiative also had the direct backing of Edwina Currie, then Secretary of State for Health.

Skills and credibility with other professionals

Secondly, senior commitment on the health professional front was felt – by both sides – to be vital in terms of gaining credibility with midwives and health professionals. 'The will to do what we are trying to do is there already – but we want to introduce new systems, create new attitudes, and re-orientate people'.

'We are amazed at the enthusiasms and interest of health professionals in doing this,' says the Joint Breastfeeding Initiative. Dora Henschel, former Director of Midwifery Services at King's College Hospital in London, was recruited by the campaign as their national co-ordinator and lead health professional, to work exclusively with health professionals as an interface between the voluntary and statutory sectors. 'We recognised that it is easier for another health professional to be sure of her ground. We are, after all, asking health professionals to question what they are doing, and some people may feel they are losing status in some way. We are also asking them to accept that even as health professionals, they have something new to learn.'

The move to employ a health professional as part of the team has 'worked very well – but partly', stresses Barbara, 'because Dora understands and empathises with the way in which voluntary bodies like us work, but also the way in which volunteers can be used'.

Hierarchical support

Dora Henschel has also taken the approach of meeting professionals and enlisting support 'from the top down' – 'we are not stressing the provision of a new service, but the use of volunteers, rotas, new approaches and flexibility. I do recognise that senior management support is important – if you can introduce things from the top it will work immediately, if you are starting below that level, without that support, it's much harder.'

To support the work of the initiative the Department of Health has issued a booklet, *The National Breastfeeding Initiative: Supporting and Promoting Breastfeeding*, and has sent this to all DHAs with a Health Circular that encourages health authorities to work with local JBI groups in furthering the project's aims. The circular acknowledges the need for support from the health authorities, and provides practical guidance on ways in which a supportive climate can be created locally: 'Authorities are asked to encourage their maternity services liaison committee to publicise the Initiative and hold training and other projects, to agree study time for Initiative projects, and to review infant feeding policies.'

Business-like approach

In supporting the JBI the Department have been fortunate in being able to draw on an already existing structure – for example, the JBI has reasonably secure premises at the NCT head office in Acton. This can occasionally bring other pressures – sharing staffing with the NCT has meant that there are occasional awkwardnesses about use of people's time, but there are commensurate benefits – for example, the NCT is able to make use of the JBI's laser printer.

The Department have recognised the need to involve other skills. Secretarial help has been provided as part of the Section 64 funding; they have adequate computer and other office equipment (including fax); and are putting in another bid for a consultant to provide permanent help with public relations and communications. Barbara Henry is unequivocal about the learning curve involved in making any organisation professional: 'It is a very great shift from being a volunteer with a commitment to breastfeeding to becoming a professional director of a high-profile and growing organisation. It has taken me some time to come to terms with all the demands on my time, and how best to organise them.'

Evaluation

The Department of Health is to embark on an evaluation of the project, looking both at 'hard' data (the levels of breastfeeding before and after the Initiative in both national and selected local districts), and 'softer' data – attitudes among health professionals and mothers, both to breastfeeding and to the Initiative.

The future

Currently the partners are doubtful that a role exists for specific contracts with GPs or health authorities (although one GP surgery has a voluntary breastfeeding counsellor employed by the practice on a regular, though very occasional, basis). More likely is the question of procurement – could DHAs support and buy into the JBI, which would supply health promotion services direct to their area? A possibility that remains to be explored.

Contact: Barbara Henry
    Chair
    Joint Breastfeeding Initiative
    Alexandra House
    Oldham Terrace
    Acton
    London W3 6NH
    Tel: 081-992 8637

Campaign Against Drinking and Driving and the Department of Transport Drink-Driving Advertising Campaign

'We see ourselves as a watchdog organisation making sure progress is gained, never lost – we'll continue to co-operate with government departments to make sure things get even better – Graham Buxton, Secretary, CADD

The partners

Voluntary sector: CADD (Campaign Against Drinking and Driving)
Statutory sector: Department of Transport

History

Dynamic and committed leadership

CADD was created in 1985 following a chance meeting between John Knight and Graham Buxton. Both had lost children as victims of drunken drivers, and both were convinced that something was 'very wrong' with the way in which such fatalities were 'treated as accidents, labelled as accidents and dealt with as such by the courts'. They resolved to mount a campaign to inform the public about the immense harm done by drunken drivers and the suffering (and consequent ill-health) cause to victims' families; to push for tougher legislation; to urge more action by police and heavier sentences by the courts, and to provide a support mechanism for grieving families. As well as this, CADD

- runs an annual conference
- produces a newsletter every quarter for members
- has produced an advice booklet for victims of drunk driving, which covers all aspects of the system, including welfare benefits
- has a range of booklets on coping with bereavement.

CADD's first appearance provoked intense interest from the media, and an overwhelming response from the public. Over 2000 families joined the organisation – victims of drunk-driving accidents, who came together to express their suffering and grief and to lobby government for action.

At the outset, CADD encountered a polite response from government, but very little active support. 'They saw us as a fringe organisation with very little campaigning power', explains Graham Buxton, 'and we in turn were faced with a government that did not want to be proactive on this issue – and by general disinterest among the public, who saw drunken driving as a joke and no more.' However, it was the beginning of a relationship between CADD and the Department of Transport.

CADD was fiercely critical of the government's annual advertising campaigns on drinking and driving: 'Quite simply, we thought it made light of a serious issue and did not adequately convey to the public the disaster to human life caused by drinking and driving.'

The mentor

When Peter Bottomley succeeded Lynda Chalker as Minister for Roads and Traffic, in 1986, the climate of help changed quite dramatically for CADD. 'The strength of feeling among our members that government was not doing enough was not lost on Mr Bottomley when he was guest speaker at our annual CADD conference in 1987,' says Graham Buxton. 'He got a very rough ride, and although he was shocked by the reception he left the meeting promising to do what he could to help us, and he did.'

Peter Bottomley's visit coincided with a change of strategy by his Department. In the summer of 1987, the Department had published *Road Safety: the Next Steps*, a policy document that set out major strategy and the target of reducing accidents by one-third by the year 2000.

Part of this strategy was to build on existing links with voluntary organisations in the field, such as Alcohol Concern and CADD; with the private sector, and with enforcement agencies like the police. A new advertising agency (Waldron, Allen, Henry & Thompson) was brought in to work on the government campaign, and a new, harder-hitting, campaign strategy emerged: 'Drinking and Driving Wrecks Lives', which concentrated on the social consequences of drinking and driving. However, despite this sea-change, both Graham Buxton and members of the Ministry feel that Peter Bottomley's personal commitment made an enormous difference. 'Although every Minister uses his energy in different ways, he was undoubtedly an enormously powerful influence in pushing forward boundaries and he really was a crusader in terms of road safety,' says Mike Ricketts, Deputy Head of Information at the Department of Transport.

Hierarchical support

During the autumn of 1987, the relationship between CADD and the DoT was firmly cemented. Summer 1987 had already seen the introduction of two television commercials on the 'wrecks lives' theme – one called 'The Fireman's Story' and one called 'The Children's Story'. Now the advertising agency had come up with a third – 'The Mother's Story', which introduced the personal dimension of someone who had lost a loved one as a result of a drink-drive accident.

Discussion between CADD and the Department over the storyline and the copy produced an offer from CADD not only to support the campaign, but, if possible, to provide one of their members who had lost a child in this way to talk to the media about their experiences. This offer was, to quote Mike Ricketts, 'one of the most radical – and helpful – gestures we have ever had from a voluntary organisation. We appreciated the enormous generosity of a victim's parent's offer to talk publicly about a very personal tragedy, and realised at once that it would give an enormous boost to the campaign'.

With CADD's support, the launch was an emotionally-charged experience. There was a huge amount of media coverage of both CADD and the campaign, and, in Graham Buxton's view, the attitude of the public changed almost overnight.

CADD also found another benefit – they were being actively sought out, both by the press, for a sharp media comment, and as a support mechanism for government.

Mutual respect

'I believe that successful partnerships are unquestionably a lot about personalities and people getting on together,' says Mike Ricketts. 'There is a lot of mutual respect between the team here at the Department and Graham and John and the other people we have come to know at CADD, and we will continue to develop the relationship in whatever way we can.' Graham Buxton agrees, 'We got a lot of support and there was a general team feeling – that if it was a success, it would be a feather in their caps as well.'

Skills and credibility with other professionals

Relationships with the police are helped by the fact that Graham Buxton was an ex-policeman – he retired from his position as deputy head of West Mercia CID in 1981. He believes that being an ex-policeman 'has been a huge help – people realise we know what we are talking about.' Graham Buxton lectures at police seminars and colleges.

Secure funding

CADD is entirely financed by donations. To date CADD has been unsuccessful in obtaining core funding from the Department of Transport. 'This is partly because of the emphasis CADD have placed upon campaigning for legislation change, and partly because victim support falls outside the definition of road safety which we are permitted to grant aid,' explains Mike Ricketts.

However, the Department has placed advertisements in CADD's newsletter and has tried to help indirectly through its advertising agency. CADD are now hopeful that their claim to being an organisation that 'promotes good health' will find favour with the Department of Health. CADD believes that credibility has been given to this view by its selection for an Evian Health Award in October 1990 'for their campaign to raise awareness of the dangerous effects of alcohol on driving behaviour.'

Business-like approach

Running a financially-secure business is one of Graham Buxton's priorities, and CADD will be making approaches to trusts and continuing to fund-raise in an effort to make its funding more secure. It falls under a peculiar 'heading' among voluntary organisations – not a registered charity but a non-profit-making company limited by guarantee, because its legal advisers felt that the central core of campaigning would not allow it to gain charitable status. There are eleven directors of CADD's limited company, who come from all over the country, and meet eight times a year. CADD now has the use of office space in Newcastle, at a favourable rent.

Evaluation

While the Department believes that drinking and driving has progressively declined since the introduction of the anti-drink driving stance in the late 1970s, CADD feels more emphatic about the positive effect of the 'wrecks lives' campaign. 'We think the figures speak for themselves – overall deaths from drunken driving were reduced dramatically after the campaign,' says Graham Buxton. CADD can point to other changes in public attitude that the campaign has brought about, including recent polls which show up to 90 per cent of the public in favour of random breath testing, and some which show 90 per cent of the public in favour of a zero limit for drivers. 'We feel it was the collaboration on that one campaign that really helped enormously.'

The future

'We are confident that support for random breath testing will continue,' says Graham Buxton, who points to the number of police forces who are themselves in favour. 'We are committed to continuing to keep up public awareness and to lobby government wherever we can – though I believe that now we have a working relationship with the Department we shall achieve a lot more by praising the good work they do than by being critical.'

Contact: Graham Buxton
          83 Jesmond Road
          Newcastle upon Tyne NE2 1NH
          Tel: 091-281 1581
          Fax: 091-281 4591

Cancercare, Lancaster

'Cancercare embodies health visiting principles as I see them' – Pippa Holdcroft, health visitor/co-ordinator, Cancercare

'We believe . . . it is possible to build an integrated team of people from the experts working in separate fields: doctors, nurses, pharmacists, social workers, dietitians (to name but a few) acting as equal colleagues; patients, relatives, volunteers and professionals all forming a comprehensive support group . . . In this way, we believe that highly technical, up-to-the-minute treatment for cancer can be carried out in a compassionate environment' (*Rapport*, Cancercare's quarterly magazine, July 1990)

The partners

Voluntary: Cancercare
             St John's Hospice
Statutory: Lancaster DHA (funding for health visitor with special responsibility for oncology; input of other health visitors; support of local hospital oncology and chemotherapy unit staff)

History

The beautiful, rolling countryside round the Lakes has a tradition of innovative and imaginative community service. It also has some of the highest levels in the country of particular cancers. Cancercare is an independent, registered charity, devoted to the support of the cancer patient and his or her family, and based at St John's Hospice in Lancaster. In November 1990 it moved into independent premises in Slynedales, in the grounds adjoining St John's Hospice.

Cancercare's main thrust is friendship, supportive advice and counselling for cancer patients and their families.

The mentor

It was started by three health professionals. Dr M. B. MacIlmurray is the consultant oncologist for the area. Appointed by the Regional Health Authority in 1978, Dr MacIlmurray's brief was to develop a district-based chemotherapy unit and out-patients clinic (previously the area was served by Christies, in Manchester, a long and tiring round-trip drive for a patient who needed chemotherapy). In 1981 Dr MacIlmurray was instrumental in getting authorisation for a health visitor attachment, with special responsibility for oncology. Pippa Holdcroft was the health visitor appointed: 'My brief was to attend outpatient clinics, follow up patients and to keep in touch with them, and to assess both patient and family needs.'

Flexible, dynamic leadership

Together with Pippa Holdcroft and Sister Sedgewick, the oncology outpatients sister, Dr MacIlmurray set up a relatives support group in premises provided by the District Health Promotion Unit. The three ran the support group in their spare time. The hard work and enthusiasm paid off: the group became self-supporting, met regularly for three years, and decided to become a registered charity to raise further funding. 'We needed the freedom', says Pippa 'and we have never lacked for generous support from the community.' Cancercare was based in St John's Hospice, a purpose-built building opened in January 1986.

The hospice is run by Sister Aine, Matron, and a team of nurses from the Order of Our Lady of Apostles, has 28 beds, and accommodates not only cancer patients, but offers respite care for patients with conditions such as multiple sclerosis.

The philosophy of the hospice is positive and flexible – 'when a patient first comes to us, we ask them what they would like to achieve while they are here. We support them in obtaining the best quality of life, and, wherever possible, to enjoy it and go home – even if it is just for a weekend or for a special occasion,' says Sister Aine. Of the terminally ill group of patients, approximately one-third are discharged. The hospice works very closely with its volunteers: 'Our whole philosophy and service has been enriched because the volunteers are there. They bring a freshness from outside to us. Where do we begin and where do we end? It's like a marriage between the hospice nursing staff and the volunteers.' (Sister Aine, St John's Hospice, July 1990)

Likewise, the hospice is flexible about staff involvement in Cancercare: Susie Roth, a nurse at the hospice, spends one morning a week running the drop-in at Kendal. And the volunteers are clear that they, too, 'get a great deal out of it'.

An increasing proportion of hospice patients have been through the service provided by Cancercare: an emphasis on building an extended family that is sharing the same burden and supporting each other, through support groups with regular evening meetings, when there is friendly chat in a relaxed and informal environment, with refreshments, entertainment such as speakers or circle dancing, and a raffle. 'The presence of doctors, health visitors and volunteers at the meetings gives members the chance to chat informally about anything that may be worrying them, or possible improvements that could be made to the service'. ('What is Cancercare?' – information sheet)

Complementary therapies such as massage, yoga, art lessons, relaxation classes, which were all held in the hospice, are now held at Slynedales. Swimming sessions are also held (at a nearby pool).

Any hospice patients well enough can, if they wish, move to the light and airy sitting-room area and join in with any of the sessions, so there is considerable overlap between hospice patients and Cancercare members, particularly those using the day-care facility. The hospice is modern, light and airy – more like a community centre than a hospital. 'Patients get to see the hospice as a part of their care that they can "dip in and out of". We work alongside the hospital on one extreme, and with Cancercare on the other. Patients and their families come to regard us as a friend, rather than an acute nursing service,' says Sister Aine. Even the casual visitor picks up the sense of serenity, warmth and friendship that pervades the hospice.

Cancercare runs the following activities:

Day care	Provided at the hospice between 10.30 and 3.30 on Monday and Thursday – patients are collected by minibus if required, manned by a rota of volunteer drivers. The day-care offers relief for carers too.
Art and craft sessions	Regular art and craft sessions are run with day-care patients: from cushion-making and simple embroidery to painting and jewellery design.
Complementary therapy	Not all health professionals locally are as positive as Cancercare's members about the role of complementary therapy, but representatives from a number of hospitals in the area have been on visits to the hospice to see the group's activities. 'Some of the medics feel there is no valid proof that it helps, but we believe that patients don't want to be bored stiff, or frightened, by their illness – they want to get on and enjoy life. In some respects, you could say that the NHS only provides those services that are "necessary to people's wellbeing" – we're providing something that the NHS would call a "luxury item".'

- massage – usually the first therapy offered to members. One masseuse combines massage with physiotherapy and relaxation which is also offered as a domiciliary service
- hypnotherapy/psychotherapy – 35 patients were seen over the last year – both at home and in the hospice
- Alexander Technique – available at the hospice once a week, and at the Kendal drop-in once a week. Two teachers are able to provide this
- relaxation – regular classes several afternoons each week
- yoga – held one afternoon a week
- swimming – offered weekly in Lancaster and Kendal at a local pool – again, the minibus can be used if needed.

Drop-ins and other groups	As well as organising therapy sessions, and providing the supportive group sessions to benefit the 'whole' patient at St John's Hospice, Cancercare runs a number of

'drop-ins' at towns around Lancaster, such as Kendal, Morecambe and Windermere. These take place one morning a week and are used by local health visitors and Macmillan nurses as an opportunity to make contact with particular patients.

One group – the Splinter Group – meets regularly to support young cancer patients between 16 and 40.

Cancercare's energies have launched two new other thriving support groups: the North Lancs Mastectomy Support Group, and the Lost Chords Club, a support group for laryngectomy patients.

Skills and credibility with other professionals

The Cancercare team has a unique liaison with the chemotherapy unit in Lancaster Hospital (in fact the organisation contributes to the staff costs for the ward). Dr MacIllmurray has a central role as the consultant attached to the ward, and apart from seeing patients at the hospital, also attends the regular Cancercare evening meetings, and visits the drop-ins. He is regarded by many patients as a friend, as well as a clinician.

The present ward sister is a volunteer worker at Cancercare's Splinter Group branch for young people with Cancer; the previous ward sister (now retired) is a volunteer worker with Cancercare.

Mutual respect

This mutual respect, friendship and close co-operation between the hospital staff and the Cancercare team at the hospice ensure there is good communication between the two. The Cancercare team (either at the hospice or at the drop-ins in Kendal or Morecambe) will encourage cancer patients to self-refer to the hospital if they believe their health has deteriorated, and there is too long for them to wait before they are next booked in to see the consultant.

The links with Cancercare also ensure that chemotherapy is tailored to fit in with families' lives. Cancercare arranged that one patient, a mother with young children, was able to schedule her chemotherapy for late on a Friday afternoon, at a time when her husband could leave work and look after her children. She could return home and rest and recover over the weekend, leaving him free to go back to work again on the Monday. Transport to and from the hospital can be arranged by a team of volunteer drivers.

Funding

Cancercare is entirely funded by donations, but an example of the generous support given is the raising of money to purchase a Cancercare minibus – by families in the tiny Cumbrian village of Betham, whose 'local' (The Wheatsheaf) organised fund-raising activities.

However, Cancercare is entering a new phase of expansion following the purchase of Slynedales, the Victorian Gothic manor next door to the hospice. Cancercare believes that Slynedales is an ideal acquisition, and teams of volunteers are helping the professional builders and decorators to make ready what will become the headquarters of Cancercare, housing complementary therapy, drop-ins, and fully staffed by a volunteer team between 10.00 am and 4.00 pm, Monday to Friday.

Fund-raising is an activity that is constantly taking place at Cancercare. Over the last year, many Cancercare members were involved in a literature project run by a writer-in residence at the hospice. Lynn Alexander's *Now I Can Tell*, a collection of poems, short articles and photographs, was published in August 1990 by Macmillan.

Cancercare's philosophy of extended supported for both patients and families has ensured a constant supply of volunteers. Patients in remission, individuals who have lost members of their families to cancer, all form an extended network: raising funds, painting the new building, driving the minibus, running the drop-ins or helping with the day-care facility.

Businesslike approach

However, Cancercare does have the benefit of a structured team who administer the organisation in a very professional way, good office facilities, and a management team with financial expertise (helping them to secure the necessary finance to purchase and refurbish Slynedales – and to buy it at auction).

They also realise the necessity of having a firm, professional structure now that the organisation is getting bigger, particularly as Cancercare wants to keep as close as possible to the needs of its members. Pippa Holdcroft, possibly the most central figure to Cancercare's continued development (and much loved and appreciated by all) is still very much involved with the running of the organisation as part of her work as an oncology health visitor.

Meg McCaldin, another key member of the team, is a salaried full-time services manager, ensuring that all the administrative functions take place, manning (with Pippa) the telephone help-line; organising fund-raising, publicity, the magazine (which now has two editors), the running of the office and liaison with all the management committees.

Susie Roth (hospice nurse), Ellie Maguire (Macmillan nurse) and Stephanie Mains (day-care) are all involved in the administration and services sub-committee of the project.

Evaluation

Evaluation of the work of Cancercare is very important to the organisation, though they have found it hard to decide how to evaluate such a very qualitative service. 'We have always believed in operating as friends – and that patients will "vote with their feet" if we don't get it right,' says Lizzie Watson, the masseuse. 'If they say it helps, then it helps' and 'life isn't always scientific' are some of the other comments that come up when evaluation is mentioned.

However, Cancercare do monitor use of their services, phone calls received, and they have been exploring, with the help of Lancaster University's Systems Unit, how to develop a framework for evaluation. This will cover the following areas:

- deciding what services are currently offered
- assessing the beneficial effects of services on patients
- participation of patients and relatives in decision-making
- obtaining resources
- use of Cancercare's name in fund-raising
- the effect of resource-attracting activities
- quality and participation of users
- opportunities for volunteers to use their skills in Cancercare
- measuring the effect of promotional activities
- reasons for non-participation of users
- effect of Cancercare in providing better patient communication.

The future

Cancercare seems stable and set for the future. Aspirations include the purchase of a Cancercare 'base' in Kendal (currently they rent the Kirland Hall for the once-a-week sessions), and the establishment there of the same kind of evening programme that takes place in Lancaster.

Contact: Pippa Holdcroft
          Cancercare
          Slynedales
          Lancaster Road
          Slyne
          Lancaster LA2 6AW
          Tel: 0524 381820

PARTNERSHIPS AIMING TO PROVIDE ACCESS

Brent Sickle Cell and Thalassaemia Centre

'What people have liked about our approach to the community is the personal contact, and being able to talk to someone who is part of the Health Service but also part of their culture. Someone who can relate both to them clinically and socially' – Dr Elizabeth Anionwu, Head of Brent Sickle Cell and Thalassaemia Centre, until July 1990

The partners

Voluntary: Brent Sickle Cell Support Group/Sickle Cell Society

Statutory: Sickle Cell Centre staff – part of Central Middlesex Hospital Trust and of the Regional Health Authority (located at the Central Middlesex Hospital)

History

It is estimated by Brozovic and Davies that there are nearly 5000 individuals in Britain affected by the inherited group of red blood conditions known as sickle cell disorders.[1] This is equal to the numbers affected by disorders such as cystic fibrosis and haemophilia.

Most – but by no means all – of those suffering from the disorder are of minority ethnic origin – usually Afro-Caribbeans or West Africans.

The Brent Sickle Cell and Thalassaemia Centre is a part of the National Health Service – a service for sickle cell sufferers at the Central Middlesex Hospital. But while it is part of the Health Service, it has become so sensitive to the needs of the local community, and merges so well with the needs of the voluntary parents' support group that overall it is seen almost as a voluntary organisation. 'The fact that the centre, based within the NHS, could be confused with a black voluntary organisation is evidence, I feel, of the traditional breaking down of barriers that exist in the Health Service,' comments Elizabeth Anionwu.

The centre relies on networking between the volunteers, patients and the organising health professionals. Its success has led to replication – within the NHS, there are sickle cell screening and counselling centres in 20 health districts.

It offers the following: *screening* of babies for the disease (as part of the Regional Health Authority's screening programme); screening of adults and anyone who requests it; *counselling* both on the effects and course of the disease; *health promotion* to combat the disease: advice on matters related to housing, access to information, financial problems and diet and nutrition.

And, with one death a year among the 400 or so registered clients, the centre also offers *bereavement counselling*.

Mutual respect

Counselling is carried out by professionals (nurses and health visitors) employed by the centre, but volunteers from the community play an important role.

The local support group meets in the centre, and the group is able to use hospital premises 'as their own', holding meetings when they want, getting photocopying done, etc. The support group is run by the parents and the affected individuals, only occasionally do the centre's counsellors go along.

'But most important of all', says Elizabeth Anionwu, 'the parents offer *us* a service. When people find out that their child has got the condition, they go through a variety of emotions – shock, anger, guilt – and we are able to say to them, we can put you in touch with parents who have gone through this. This also applies to at-risk couples – couples who are not really sure what decision they want to make [about having children who may have the condition].'

Through its history, the accent has been on being 'driven' by the needs of the community.

Elizabeth Anionwu again: 'It was agreed that the centre should be in a health setting if blood tests were to be easily available, but that it should be geographically located within easy access of the at-risk community and not be based in a large hospital. Additionally there should be an open-door policy that would not require a rigid appointment system or a letter from a doctor. Individuals could self-refer, and the counsellor and clerical staff should be in a position to arrange the standard blood tests required. Every effort was made to avoid people having to make repeated journeys to the centre. Cards would be issued in order to accommodate the overwhelming request that people be promptly and accurately informed about the results of their blood tests. Clients would also be asked if they would agree to their results being sent to their general practitioners.'[2]

The centre has also run very successful training courses aimed at people going out into the field – midwives, health visitors, even a few doctors: 'It's not only to tell people what sickle cell is, but to highlight counselling techniques, and the day-to-day implications of having the condition.' The courses have always been multi-disciplinary – a factor appreciated by those who have attended. 'It's great to have such a mix of people on the course,' said a recent course evaluation note.

Enthusiastic dynamic leadership

The Brent Sickle Cell Centre was set up ten years ago, on the impetus of two pioneering women who encountered each other working in the hospital. Milica Brozovic was a consultant haematologist in the hospital, who had an interest in what was then an unfashionably rare disease confined to a small, unvocal minority, and Elizabeth Anionwu, a community nurse tutor at the hospital, who was also an active member of the local black community. Elizabeth Anionwu recalls: 'I realised that I was ignorant about the condition, and I wasn't really able to do anything to help affected families who were on my health visiting list. I felt pretty helpless. It struck me then that if there had been a voluntary organisation, I would have been able to get more support for the family – for instance, if the child has cystic fibrosis or diabetes, as a health visitor you can tap into a network.'

Such a voluntary organisation was not to appear until 1975, when OSCAR was set up. In 1977, a local support group was formed for those affected by the disease. There were a number of reasons for this initial impetus – the death of a colleague from leukaemia; the comment of a friend who said 'if people like you [i.e. health professionals] don't know anything about this, how are we supposed to?'; and a series of lunchtime seminars given by Dr Brozovic in the hospital to inform health professionals about sickle cell anaemia and what it meant.

Hierarchical support in the hospital

Milica Brozovic and Elizabeth Anionwu formed an informal partnership in the hospital to raise the level of awareness of the disease and to co-ordinate the care of patients: from easing stress and isolation on the wards, to providing information – which was lacking from other sources – about the illness, how it was likely to run, and what caused it.

'I became aware that there was no information on the health promotion side, and when I visited relatives in the States I became aware of this concept called a sickle cell centre – a mixture of screening and counselling,' recalls Elizabeth Anionwu. Over several summers she made holiday visits to Los Angeles, the centre of sickle cell activity in the United States, and became more and more aware of the health promotion work being done there, and the materials that could be made available.

The mentor

In 1979, with Dr Brozovic's support, a two-year grant, of £10 000 a year, was obtained from the North West Thames Regional Health Authority, to identify, first of all, whether there was a need for such a centre.

Elizabeth Anionwu is very positive about the usefulness of a senior member of staff to support and legitimise the project: 'It's no good working in isolation, because you've got to have somebody within the infrastructure who knows the mechanism for obtaining funding – or even for obtaining statistics. You've got to try and press your case against all the other competing groups. You need someone of senior status to back your case – a senior registrar, or someone senior in the public health field.'

Funding

The centre is now mainly financed by North West Thames Regional Health Authority, and the 1987 programme to screen new-born babies for the disease has allowed a small further expansion in the counselling and office staff.

Relationships with GPs

The centre is well known – partly because it has always attracted publicity and has therefore had a high profile with local and national media. Every group practice in Brent was made aware of the centre some time ago – flooded with leaflets and posters, and responses from GPs have encouraged active referrals to the centre.

Evaluation

The centre has counted attendance and monitored self-referral patterns (there is an encouraging level of 50 self-referrals).

The future

Elizabeth Anionwu left in July 1990. What impact that will have on the running of the centre remains to be seen. The centre has undoubtedly been very successful, and has grown into a large organisation, and she wonders whether it has grown too large: 'Being a regional laboratory is fine, but the centre is in danger of growing too big to serve the community in the best possible way.'

Instead, she would like to see the creation of more such centres, placed within the community. Of the twenty centres now set up and running in the UK, seven are sited in hospitals, eleven are sited within health centres, only one (Lambeth) is purpose-built within the community, and one (Wolverhampton) is based in a community church hall: 'I think in Brent we have become somewhat isolated because we have become too medicalised, but it's part of the management structure. We should be part of the community health service – in fact, all the other counselling centres in the UK are part of the primary health care team. Historically, we asked to be part of the community healthcare system too, but ten years ago we were ahead of our time.'

Contact: Brent Sickle Cell Centre
Central Middlesex Hospital
Acton Lane
London NW10 7NS
Tel: 081-453 2262/2685

References

1. M. Brozovic and S. C. Davies, 'Management of sickle cell disease', *Postgraduate Medical Journal*, vol. 63, 1987, 605–9.
2. E. Anionwu, 'Community development approaches to sickle cell anaemia', *Talking Point* (Association of Community Workers), May 1990.

Further reading

E. Anionwu, 'Running a sickle cell centre: community counselling', in *Ethnic Factors in Health and Disease* ed. J. K. Cruikshank and P. G. Beevers. Wright: Butterworth, 1989.

West Yorkshire Travellers Project

The partners

Statutory sector: Leeds East Health Authority
Leeds West Health Authority
Voluntary sector: Save the Children Fund

Background

The West Yorkshire Travellers Project was set up in April 1988 as a result of discussion between Save the Children Fund (SCF) and the two health authorities. It has the following aims:

- to assist Travellers, the local settled population and local services to find common solutions to the discrimination and disadvantage experienced by Travellers in Leeds and neighbouring authorities
- to support Travellers in negotiating full access to local services, and in particular to health services, and appropriate provision to meet their needs.

There are 56 official sites for Travellers in Leeds and the surrounding areas; with a Traveller population of 80 to 120 families there is a natural shortfall of official places for Travellers. Because of this, many families are evicted and forced to move to unofficial sites, which makes it difficult for them to maintain continuity in health care and education and to make links in the immediate community. Many Traveller children under 5 in the Leeds area are living on unofficial sites, often in conditions which the project regards as 'unhealthy and dangerous'.

Overall financial control of the project rests with SCF's North and East Divisional Office, who also have the objective of making sure that any initiatives to tackle the problems faced by Travellers are joint initiatives between the voluntary and statutory sectors.

Save the Children Fund also pays for a project co-ordinator, with Leeds City Council funding the cost of a project worker through its Urban Programme. Leeds Eastern and Western Health Authorities jointly provide half the funding for the post of special health visitor, who is based with other health visitors in the health centre nearest to the official site, and who works exclusively with the project. Apart from ensuring regular contact with the special health visitor, the partnership agreement also sets out that SCF and the two health authorities will share and exchange any relevant training resources – 'the project budget has provided training experiences for the health visitor which may not have been possible otherwise,' says Therese Griffiths, the project co-ordinator.

All agencies involved in the project have to agree on staff taken on to work for the project.

Activities

So far, the project has undertaken all the usual work of health visiting, with an emphasis on women's health and health education. Other areas covered are welfare rights – advocacy – liaison with other agencies; both on behalf of individual Travellers and addressing issues; a women's group; training for others on working with Gypsies and Travellers.

Working together

At the outset of the project, it was decided to draw up an official partnership agreement. This is standard procedure for SCF and both health authorities. This formality has proved to be a positive help to the project, says Therese, 'inasmuch as because it's there, we don't need to lean on it.'

In particular, the agreement is explicit about the parameters for the participating agencies. It says 'SCF will undertake that no member of their staff will substitute for statutory services or in any way undermine the operation of such services. SCF will avoid creating long-term dependence on SCF staff and resources . . . The statutory agencies with special responsibility for Travellers will not request an SCF staff member to undertake duties that are properly the responsibility of a statutory body.'

The agreement also covers the questions of complaints about health authority or SCF staff; grievances and commendations. The possibility of disagreement between the partners is also covered (although this has never been the case), with the ultimate sanction that if agreement between the parties is not reached, 'the partners can choose to end the partnership by majority vote.'

While SCF does not have a standard form for such partnerships, 'we have learnt from experience', says Therese. 'The agreement is rarely referred to, but we are aware of it in our dealings.'

Support for the project

There is a named line manager acting for both health authorities.

Mutual respect

The health authorities say: 'The partnership makes provision for formal meetings between the agencies offering us an opportunity to agenda items for discussion. Many benefits have accrued to the partnership from the agencies involved – these include a much better induction and training for the health visitor than would have been possible without the association with SCF.'

Both partners point out: 'In addition to the formal partnership meetings, the SCF staff line manager and the health visitors' line manager have held informal meetings to update each other on developments. This has worked quite well and been quite helpful not only as a means of keeping informed, but in promoting a sense of working together.'

Save the Children comment, 'The partnership has undoubtedly offered us greater opportunities to influence systems than we would otherwise have enjoyed. It is fair to say that we have grown into working together and methods have been established for future joint work on the project.'

Evaluation

There is internal evaluation with external support, paid for by Save the Children Fund. 'Early drafts of the evaluation', says Therese Griffiths, 'show that the project appears to be successful locally,' and 'we are particularly pleased with the success of the health visiting service, the women's group, and the training we are providing for other agencies.'

Contact: Annie Franklin
         Principal Officer
         Save the Children Fund
         North and East Divisional Office
         2nd Floor
         National Deposit House
         1 Eastgate
         Leeds LS2 7LY
         Tel: 0532 424823

HEALTHY CITIES

The UK Health for All Network

The UK Health for All Network (formerly Healthy Cities) includes not just health professionals, but anyone with a responsibility for health in its broadest sense, e.g. environmental health, housing, planning, education and social services, and voluntary bodies, working together in local Health for All partnerships. Its objectives are to develop a healthy public policy, share information, commission and undertake research, and organise conferences. The network includes a number of towns and boroughs, and (at the end of 1990) had a mailing list of 350 supporting the initiative.

The network is based on the philosophy of Health for All. 'The chief underlying principle is that equity in health is achievable and that gaps in health status between and within communities can be lessened. The second underlying principle is that of multi-sectoral collaboration. Good health was once thought to be the sole responsibility of health services and the individual. It is now recognised that the work of all statutory agencies, industries and communities affect our health.' (Hull Healthy Cities Initiative report)

There is also commitment to the principle of community participation – of enabling local people to define their own health needs and priorities and to work in partnership to develop a local healthy public policy.

Funding

Funding for the network originally came from the HEA, with help from Liverpool City Council, who have so far covered staffing and office costs, telephone and postage for the co-ordinator, Marie Armitage (based in Liverpool). However, it is now entering an era when it is expected to become more self-supporting, and has consciously taken the decision that although most of its members come from (or are employed by) the statutory sector, it will decide on a constitution and become a voluntary organisation, with a membership which encourages participation by all sectors. It is hoped that this will allow it to raise funds towards increased training, breaking down the boundaries between the different sectors and sharing problems and experiences, and information.

The network also hopes to create a post that would act as a point of contact for anyone seeking information on the local implementation of the Health for All philosophy. 'Deciding on a constitution has not been easy,' comments Marie Armitage, 'but has proved a very useful exercise in agreeing common aims and objectives for the network.'

Aims

The network is guided by a number of principles:

- health defined as social, physical and mental wellbeing
- local collaboration between all agencies, particularly the local authorities, health authorities, voluntary and community groups; with other statutory agencies, academic institutions, industrial and commercial organisations, trades unions and professional bodies being involved whenever possible
- community participation
- empowering people both individually and collectively
- accountability to the public and service users
- equal opportunities and taking discrimination into account
- primary health care (which begins with the family and community)
- public services directed towards promoting health
- national and international co-operation.

Commitment

With such principles, commitment is high on the list of priorities, and the location and status of those appointed by local authorities to work as Healthy City co-ordinators varies considerably. Some cities have chosen to appoint very senior health service staff, as a sign of their commitment to policy changes in the health authority. Others, however, have recognised how difficult it can be to work across the local authority/health authority boundary, and one or two cities have chosen to find another way of working by siting the post *in the voluntary sector* – and giving the person in charge the task, *from that vantage point*, of co-ordinating work across all three sectors: voluntary, health authority and local authority.

Contact: Marie Armitage
          UK Health for All Network
          PO Box 101
          Liverpool L69 5BE
          Tel: 051-231 1009
          Fax: 051-225 2909

Hull Healthy City Initiative

'We aim to make Hull a healthier city for all its residents' – Lynn Holdridge, Co-ordinator, Hull Healthy City Initiative

HULL HEALTHY CITY

The partners

Voluntary sector:	Hull Council for Voluntary Service
Statutory sector:	Hull Health Authority
	University of Hull
	Hull City Council
	Humberside County Council
	Hull City Environmental Health Office
Other partners:	The Church of England

History

The Hull Healthy City Initiative began as the result of a joint initiative between key individuals in the health authority and the City Council. Joint finance (three years from the financial year 1989/90) was obtained, although the project is also partly funded by Inner Area Programme funds from the Department of the Environment.

Mentoring

The project enjoys very high level support, with the steering group including the chairman of the health authority, the leader of Hull City Council, a consultant in public health medicine, and local dignitaries such as the Bishop of Hull. The project is based in the Central Policy Unit at Hull City Council Offices, which gives it access to key council networks. The co-ordinator, Lynn Holdridge, and her assistant Lynn McTighe, have been in post since late 1989, and in September 1990 they were joined by a third team member – a Community Health Development Facilitator – Sheila Jones. It has been a deliberate policy to create all posts at a senior level, to give the project status within the council structure.

Lynn Holdridge sees being sited in the Central Policy Unit – rather than in the Environmental Health Department, say – as a definite advantage for a Healthy Cities Project: 'In a city like Hull, where the council structure is rather rigid, it gives us access to networks within the Council, and enables us to know what is going on. It means that the concept of Healthy City will be *central* to developing policy, rather than being marginalised.' The support of her immediate manager, Dr John Papworth, head of the council's Policy Unit, is clearly important to this, and the Healthy Cities office has already been called upon to provide input to council policy which has not traditionally been thought of as 'health-related' – for example, the project had a central involvement in devising the recent Hull Environment Charter, and has also been involved in giving advice to the council for its 'alcohol at work' policy. 'We are now actively involved in developing a broad-based food policy which is designed to target not only employees but also users of council services. This is a real development for Hull City Council,' says Lynn Holdridge.

Aims

Like other Healthy Cities projects, this initiative is based on Health for All, support for the WHO targets, and the principles of multi-sectoral collaboration. Hull Healthy City aims 'to encourage all sectors of the city to work together for a healthier Hull and to encourage communities to become involved in shaping their health.'[1]

Key objectives are:

- to raise awareness of the Healthy City Initiative
- to co-ordinate and facilitate working party activities and projects set up as part of the Healthy City Initiative

- to work with the Healthy Cities Network and support group
- to facilitate the development of healthy public policy
- to liaise with the media.

Initiatives since September 1989

Networking

The project has supported the creation of the Hull Play Council – a combination of statutory-based workers in a voluntary group setting. HHC has had input into the Hull Play Council's 'Play Charter' and has also provided publicity and funding.

Supporting individual projects/groups

HHC has £12 000 in grant moneys to give away in the financial year 1990/91, and will have £3000 in the following year. Moneys are earmarked for small community-based projects which fit with the 'Health for All' philosophy. These can either be led by the community or by the voluntary sector. The Community Health Development Facilitator will be working with others on the development of a Health Action Area in East Hull. All project moneys will be directed to groups in this area.

Creating new groups

Intersectoral working is a vital thread of HHC. One example of ways in which the HHC project is bringing together different groups of people is the Accident Prevention Forum. This is a group that includes both voluntary and statutory bodies – Pre-School Playgroups Association, Council for Voluntary Service, the police, the fire brigade, the road safety officer and the Red Cross – to look at various safety issues, for instance the sale of matches to children.
   'We have arranged the first meeting of the Hull Health Forum – a multi-sectoral group of people who have a community health brief,' says Lynn Holdridge, 'hopefully it will bring people together to share information and skills.'

Women's health group

A (struggling) women's health group in one inner-city part of Hull is being facilitated and supported by the project. It is hoped that the arrival of the new Community Health Development Facilitator will give this project a boost.

Core health indicators

HHC is trying to provide a 'snapshot' of health in Hull, showing particularly the inequalities. A number of groups are involved in this, including the FHSA, the Health Authority, the Social Services and Housing Departments.

The focus will be the same as Health for All – preventive rather than curative. HHC perceives the need to log a health profile of the city in order to measure change and to set out a health strategy for the city. The end result will, it is hoped, be both for internal and external consumption.

Lynn Holdridge adds, 'A consideration of core health indicators has shown how inadequate our "outcome" measures of health are. We would like to develop measures of health rather than morbidity and mortality!'

'Hull Daily Mail' sponsorship of play about tranquillisers

This play, sponsored by *Hull Daily Mail*, was produced for both an inner-city and a rural audience.

'Healthy Shopping Basket'

Of all the work carried out over the first year of Hull Healthy City, this project has attracted the most attention. Started with a £5000 grant from the Health Education Authority's Look After Your Heart (LAYH) programme, it was created to encourage healthy eating in the face of evidence that people on lower incomes eat less healthily – examples of research quoted by HHC include *Jam Tomorrow* from Manchester University Food Policy Unit, and the London Food Commission's *Tightening Belts* (1986). A particular aim of the project was to steer people away from the consumption of saturated fats, which have been linked with heart disease.

The Healthy Shopping Basket scheme aims 'to make healthier dietary choices the easier choices for all people in the area regardless of their social class or where they shop', by

- highlighting healthy staple foods present on most supermarket shelves
- highlighting low budget healthlier foods
- raising awareness about healthy eating
- encouraging inner-city stores to stock a wider range of healthier foods
- encouraging competitive pricing of healthier foods
- reducing confusion about which foods are healthier.

The working party on the initiative included statutory and CHC members, college of further education and church members.

Hull Healthy City achieved a link with Grandways supermarkets, a Yorkshire-based chain with 30 branches in the Humberside area alone. Costs were shared between the Healthy Shopping Basket Project and Grandways, with the HEA grant funding production of certificates for participating stores and recipe leaflets. Grandways supported the promotion with in-store channel tickets and is planning to reprint the recipe leaflets when stocks run low.

The scheme was launched in July 1990 and although still in pilot stage, there are indications that take-up of leaflets and healthy shopping items has been good. There are plans for in-store staff training so that customers can be more fully informed about the idea of the Healthy Shopping Basket.

Evaluation of the success of the project is currently being based on leaflet numbers, the idea of exit questionnaires to shoppers having been rejected as too difficult and costly to implement. (Lynn Holdridge has produced an information pack and an interim report on the initiative, both of which are available direct from the HHC office, price £2.50.)

'We are examining the possibility of developing the healthy eating approach by looking at the feasibility of food co-operatives or community-based bulk buy, which we think is an exciting potential development,' says Lynn.

Evaluation

Evaluation of the HHC project is currently in the form of setting objectives, and measuring success by the numbers of groups helped or formed, and the amount of activities carried out. There will also be a monitoring of any perceived changes/effects at DHA level. 'When we started we were seen as a cost rather than as a benefit,' says Lynn Holdridge, 'but we are here to take action, to get away from established practice, and to get people to understand that health should equal "well-ness".'

Reference

1. L. Holdridge, *Healthy City Interim Report*. Hull Healthy City Initiative, Hull, 1990.

Further reading

Hull Healthy City Initiative: First Annual Report. October 1990. Available from Hull Healthy City Initiative, price £2.50.

Contact: Ms Lynn Holdridge
Hull Healthy City Initiative
c/o Central Policy Unit
Hull City Council
The Guildhall
Alfred Gelder Street
Hull HU1 2AA
Tel: 0482 595024

*PARTNERSHIPS
ADOPTING A
COMMUNITY
APPROACH*

The partners

Statutory sector: North Derbyshire Health Promotion Service
Bolsover Community Mental Health Team
Community Education
Derbyshire Rural Community Council

*Bolsover Community Mental
Health Roadshow*

Voluntary sector: Bolsover Self-Help Network
(Agoraphobia Group; the Buckle Club;
Creswell Open Door; 1 to 3; Share;
Whitwell Self-Help Group)
Ault Hucknall Parish Church

Background

Bolsover is a rural district in the north of Derbyshire, with a total population of about 77 000 spread over at least 300 square miles. The largest town is Bolsover itself, which has a population of about 25 000 people.

Early in 1989 Bolsover Community Mental Health Team and North Derbyshire Health Promotion Service decided to have a roadshow to educate people about stress, and to show positive images of how to create good mental health. The idea was then presented to the local planning group for mental health and representatives from voluntary and statutory organisations were invited to work together to plan the event. While a separate budget for the event was 'almost non-existent', the Health Promotion Service was able to print materials produced by joint efforts, and provide a trailer to stage the roadshow, which was staffed by a team of volunteers, a member of the Health Promotion Service and members of the Community Mental Health Team.

The roadshow was chosen as a format to take the idea of positive mental health to as many people as possible. Rural Derbyshire is very short of places to meet, and transport is a problem. The Buckle Club, one of the voluntary organisations involved, has found that hiring a room for meetings is its greatest expenditure. The group needed to find a place to meet regularly which is suitable and cheap.

The statutory and voluntary partners worked together for several months to plan the roadshows. The aims were:

- to promote positive, good mental health and thus orientate the roadshow to focus on promoting mental wellbeing
- to publicise the services and groups available within Bolsover District for people needing help and support with mental health problems
- to work towards the de-stigmatisation of mental health problems, and to have information available on mental health problems
- to help identify gaps in the provision of services and to help with future planning.

The roadshow travelled on board the borrowed health authority trailer, visiting six areas: Clowne, Glapwell, Shirebrook, Bolsover, Creswell and Tibshelf during September 1989. The largest turnout for the caravan was in Clowne, with smaller numbers of people attending in more rural villages.

'Although there was not a huge turnout,' said Sylvia Young from the Health Promotion Service, 'we considered the venture to be a success. We know that people associate mental health with mental illness and fear prevents people from asking for information or support. Events of this kind begin to challenge prejudice – but it's a slow process.'

One of the difficulties encountered by the group was that suitable materials promoting positive images of mental health were very difficult to find. It was most cost-effective to produce much of their own materials, which they were able to do with the help of the Health Promotion Service staff. Publicity and siting the caravan in just the right location, were also learning areas for the future – 'Next time we will use the trailer at gala days, fêtes and similar events with, perhaps, a more family and fun atmosphere,' said Darrell Evans from Bolsover Community Mental Health Team. But, despite the difficulties, the group did find working together to be a useful experience.

One of the key volunteers, Sue Price from the Buckle Club, which meets as a social support group for people with a wide range of problems, felt that without the support of the statutory services, 'it would have been impossible for us to get things done.'

The Health Promotion Service has a policy of working with voluntary agencies, and of helping them wherever possible within the constraints of their budget. Because the locality is spread over a wide area, a new mechanism has been set up to develop health promotion in a way that is relevant to the local population. Locality Health Promotion Action Groups are being created, one in each locality of North Derbyshire. The groups will include both a voluntary sector and a statutory sector dimension, with representatives from the health authority, Social Services, trade unions, a key local voluntary organisation, and from Community Education. The network of groups was set up in May 1990, after a seminar designed to brief the participants thoroughly in defining their objectives.

Support

The Director of Public Health for the district, and the Director of Health Promotion believe that 'a lot of good things are happening in North Derbyshire', and are very supportive of working with the voluntary sector. A lot of work is being done from both the voluntary and statutory sectors on working together.

The future

Partly as a result of working on the roadshow, the Health Promotion Service have recognised that working together in partnership is the only way to ensure that services are acceptable and accessible to local people. It is important to involve representatives from the voluntary sector within the planning process and to provide adequate support and resources to facilitate consultation. The Service is, therefore, currently trying to raise awareness of the need for a paid worker to facilitate the consultative process. It is desirable to have a worker in each district to:

- Liaise with local groups and voluntary organisations which address the health concerns of their members
- Research and identify the needs of sections of the community which are not yet represented by local organisations
- Organise representation from the voluntary sector on joint planning groups
- Involve community groups/voluntary organisations in the consultation process
- Organise/facilitate meetings which bring together appropriate local groups
- Facilitate links between voluntary sector representatives on joint planning groups and the wider voluntary sector in their area.

Contact: Sylvia Young
North Derbyshire Health Promotion Service
Scarsdale Hospital
Newbold Road
Chesterfield
Derbyshire
Tel: (0246) 231255 ext. 277

Glyndon Health Project

Glyndon Health Project
Part of Greenwich Health Rights Project

'As with all voluntary projects, funding is our constant worry. Despite all our work with the health authority, we are not funded by them. Our LBG grant is frozen because of poll tax capping, and we are awaiting the outcome of a round of charitable trust applications. We could close in October 1990,* even though we seem to have broken through a number of institutional barriers and established our credibility in some areas, and are even being consulted by some service managers on specific issues' – Myra Garrett, Co-ordinator, Glyndon Health Project, August 1990

The partners

Voluntary sector: Glyndon Health Project. Currently: Neera Deepak, Asian fieldworker; Myra Garrett, Co-ordinator (17½ hours per week); Ha Nguyet Ta, Vietnamese fieldworker (17½ hours); Deborah Loeb, Community Development Health Worker (17½ hours). Deborah's post is funded by the London Borough of Greenwich – the other posts are funded by a combination of moneys from the King's Fund, City Parochial and Baring Foundations, and the London Borough Grants Scheme.

Statutory sector: Greenwich Health Authority (health professionals work alongside project workers on a number of initiatives, but no funding is provided), London Borough of Greenwich (one whole-time equivalent post plus running costs).

* See Stop Press, p. 102

Background

After the publication of the Black Report on inequalities in health (in 1980),[1] Greenwich Community Health Council held a public meeting to discuss the implications of the report for Greenwich. One of the outcomes of this meeting was a recognition that very little was known about inequalities in health in Greenwich.[2]

It was proposed that the Community Health Council should try and establish a project in a small area of Greenwich to examine various aspects of health, and to encourage local people themselves to improve their health. In 1984, the local borough council gave funding for the post of project worker for the Greenwich Health Rights Project (which became known from 1986 as the Glyndon Health Project). The project's aims were and still are:

- to enable local people in one area of Greenwich to identify their health needs, evaluate their services and press for improvements
- to encourage better use of existing NHS services
- to encourage the provision of more appropriate services
- to help people become more aware of the relation of health to the environment (for example, health and safety at work, housing, stress and lifestyle).

The initial funding for the project was for one worker for one year only and it was decided that the Glyndon ward of the London Borough of Greenwich should be used for a small survey of local people's health needs and the effect of social and material environment on their health. The findings of the survey were published in 1985 in a report *Health and Glyndon*[3] (and were still being quoted extensively in Greenwich Health Authority's 1988 Public Health Report *Life and Death in Greenwich*),[4] which talks of the 'consistently high level of deprivation in one particular ward, Glyndon' which led to an investigation being undertaken into the health of its residents. The main findings of the investigation were that:

- the health of residents of Glyndon and their children was found to be poorer than that of residents in other city areas in London and indeed nationally
- a significant group of respondents had problems with their mental health
- occupation appeared to have a direct impact on health
- low incomes had an adverse effect on health
- housing had an adverse effect on health, with greater levels of stress particularly in those living in high rise council estates than in those who owned their own property
- personal lifestyles adversely affected respondents' health in a variety of ways. One third of the respondents were overweight. The proportion of Glyndon residents who smoked was higher than nationally, and women, and not men, were more likely to be heavy drinkers compared to residents in a national study.
- while there appeared to be fairly widespread awareness of health education messages, working-class respondents appeared to be less likely to feel they could do as much to influence their health as middle-class respondents did

- Glyndon residents reported a higher use of hospitals for themselves and their children than is found nationally and this was likely to be related to high levels of morbidity, historical dependence on hospital services in Greenwich and inadequate or inappropriate provision of community and prevention services
- the take-up of health services by Asian residents was further limited by lack of information and the provision of services in appropriate manner, place and language.

The Glyndon Health project was set up at the Glyndon Community Health Council, and moved to offices above shops in Plumstead High Street in 1989.

Activities

Starting in 1985 a number of initiatives have been carried out, from large-scale projects (described below) to smaller, shorter-term projects such as a group for women with eating problems (from 1987 to March 1989); a series of short courses on holistic health, including homoeopathy, massage, stress management and relaxation (with tutors provided by the local adult education institute); a first-aid course; new mums' coffee morning; assertion training course, and 'coping with the summer holidays' sessions. Other investigations into the health care facilities of the area have also been undertaken, including:

- interviews with 16 local GPs
- encouragement of better practice premises
- encouragement of better practice information
- patients' participation in training for GP receptionists.

Glyndon Mother and Baby Clinic

This is a community-based child health clinic where there is very close collaboration with health authority staff (health visitors, and clinical medical officers). It is held weekly in the Glyndon Community Centre and attended by an average of 50 mothers each session. A project worker attends to give advice on a range of issues. Glyndon Health Project was instrumental in getting the clinic re-located to the Community Centre, and the success of this clinic was documented in a report by G. and J. Betts.[5] Despite recent staff shortages the clinic continues to be one of the best used in the district.

Parenting skills course and adult education institutes

Several short programmes aimed at offering the opportunity to discuss the issues people face in bringing up children have been well received. A ten-week course, run one day a week at the Glyndon Community Centre, was developed in consultation with the Women and Health Group. Crèche hours were provided by the local adult education institute, which also provided a tutor to run the course jointly with a project worker. The first course ran from January to March 1990, and was attended by ten women – it was so successful that it will be run again in September 1990 as part of the main adult education programme on a scaled-down basis, i.e. half-a-day sessions. A Section 64 bid to extend work with isolated parents is pending.

Work with black and ethnic communities – health promotion project with ethnic elders

A six-month health promotion programme for Asian and Vietnamese elders was initiated in September 1988, with funding from three trusts: King's Fund, City Parochial Foundation and the Baring Foundation. The project was designed following extensive consultation with people in the community. The programme covered eighteen topics in thirty-eight sessions, with the project's bilingual fieldworkers facilitating sessions with health professionals, including cervical smears and eye testing. Along with information sessions, the project began activity sessions – Tai Chi for the Vietnamese and yoga and swimming for Asian women. Again, the help of the adult education institute has proved invaluable – the institute provided tutors for these sessions. The Health Project is also extending its remit and is encouraging other elderly day centres and luncheon clubs to introduce health promotion sessions. An Asian sheltered unit (the Asra Housing Association) has launched one such scheme – where the twenty to twenty-five elders have been meeting weekly for a whole-day session including yoga, cooking and eating a healthy meal, and taking part in a health information session run by the project worker and various health professionals (such as health visitors, chiropodist, physiotherapist).

Transcultural bereavement counselling group

Awareness of the unmet needs of the bereaved in black and ethnic communities in Greenwich arose from work the project carried out with ethnic elders. A working group of around twenty members of the local Asian, Chinese/Vietnamese and African Caribbean communities has been meeting for over a year to examine local needs, with the result that training for line managers in statutory services was identified as being needed. Small amounts of funding from Greenwich Social Services Training Department helped pay for a Workshop on Transcultural Bereavement Awareness in October 1990, to increase awareness among managers of care staff of different cultural and religious death and bereavement practices in Greenwich communities, with the hope that this will cascade to a number of groups of care staff. Various funding applications are pending to develop this work.

Glyndon Health and Fitness Fair

September 1989 saw a 'fun' day on health fitness in and around Glyndon Community Centre. In partnership with the health services and local authority, some forty-five stalls, including mobile units were set up. There were 'taster' sessions on yoga, stress management and homoeopathy. Healthy food, a crèche, and entertainment were also on offer, and 750 people attended the fair. 'We confirmed that health promotion can be very popular indeed if carried out very locally in a family setting,' comments Myra Garrett. Proposals were made that this could become an annual event in the 'stress areas', with major support from the statutory authorities.

Community café

The project took on the cooking and selling of a 'healthy' lunch once a week at the Glyndon Community Centre with help from two volunteers. The success of this venture has encouraged the centre's coffee bar to be more health orientated in the kind of food it sells, and there are plans to develop this idea further.

Working with GPs

The project would like to work more closely with local GPs, and some nurses from one or two practices approach the project regularly for consultation and advice. One issue, raised recently by the FHSA, is whether they are 'professionally qualified'.

The mentor

Dr Gervase Hamilton, Greenwich's former Director of Public Health, has been very supportive of the project – including extracts from the Glyndon report in the District's Public Health Report, and his support – although only verbal – has been valuable to the project. There has also been keen support from other insiders, who have encouraged the project to try to build links with budget-holders in the health authority in the hope of securing funding for specific project-related pieces of work, 'but none of this has produced any funding as yet!' says Myra Garrett. Other health professionals in the area are using the service – 'All front line professionals have been extremely co-operative and keen to collaborate,' she adds. 'Many, such as health visitors, want to develop their health promotion work and are interested in working with us on group work and outreach.'

Evaluation

Glyndon, like many projects, is struggling to carry out meaningful evaluation. They see it as a separate skill, and have realised its importance but do not believe they currently have the resources to do it properly. Consequently, it forms an integral part of the new bids for funding they are making.

Specific project work – for example, the Health and Fitness Fair and the Ethnic Elders Health Promotion Programme, have been internally evaluated and written up.

The future

Despite being a successful and positive project, in July 1990 the future for Glyndon looked grim. One application for funding had been turned down, and while there was still funding till the end of the financial year from the London Borough of Greenwich for one worker's post, the three other staff have been given notice of impending redundancy.

Stop Press!

In a letter to the project worker in November 1990, Myra Garrett provided an update on how things were looking for Glyndon: 'Funding for two-and-a-half years has been agreed by the Regional Primary Care Development Fund for a Vietnamese Advocacy Project, which will involve research into primary care use and satisfaction, training for health staff and direct work with primary care providers on health promotion issues. Charity Projects made an award for our Ethnic Elders Adviser to develop a network of pensioners' groups and work around policy and service provision over a two-year period. Redundancy notices have been withdrawn!'

References

1. *Inequalities in Health: Report of a Research Working Group* [the Black Report]. Department of Health and Social Security, 1980. (See also Peter Townsend, Nick Davidson and Margaret Whitehead (eds), *Inequalities in Health: 'The Black Report' and 'The Health Divide'*. Penguin Books, 1988.)
2. *Glyndon Annual Report 1986/87.*
3. G. Betts. *Health and Glyndon.* Greenwich Community Health Council, 1985.
4. *Life and Death in Greenwich* (Public Health Report 1988). Greenwich Health Authority, 1988.
5. G. Betts and J. Betts. 'Establishing a child health clinic in a deprived area', *Health Visitor*, vol. 63, no. 4, April 1990.

Contact: Myra Garrett
Glyndon Health Project
106 Plumstead High Road
London SE18 1SJ
Tel: 081-854 2966

Cambridge Community Development Health Project

A health programme with a community perspective – centred on two estates in Cambridge

The partners

Voluntary sector: East Barnwell Estate (residents' association, women's health group, practice participation association)
King's Hedges Estate (residents' association, women's health group, elderly group)

Statutory sector: Cambridge Health Promotion Service
Health visitors and other members of Cambridge
DHA Primary Care Team

History

The project was originally conceived in 1985, when the Health Promotion Service, together with Cambridge City Council, put forward a joint proposal for the project.

It 'grew out of a desire on the part of Cambridge Health Authority's Health Promotion Service to investigate the effectiveness of community development approaches to health education in the context of the NHS',[1] and was modelled on the philosophy of Health for All, with a prime aim of redressing inequalities of access to health within two specific identified communities in Cambridge: King's Hedges and East Barnwell. Specific objectives included 'to identify local health concerns and needs of local people as expressed by local people, to identify and work with community networks to stimulate and extend them and to develop and contribute to co-ordinated programmes involving all the relevant local (including voluntary) agencies'. The project included an objective to carry out action research methods of evaluation. (The approaches used are described fully in *Community Development Health Project: a Review of Achievements So Far*.[1] A video and the project report, *Health is Catching* are also available.)[2]

Funding was granted in 1986, and the project started in 1987, with the appointment of two Community Health Development workers, Rosemary Cox and Gail Findlay. Rosemary was based in the King's Hedges area, within a community house; Gail was attached to the GP practice at East Barnwell Health Centre. Both workers also had a base at the health promotion unit in Addenbrooke's Hospital, Cambridge, where the project could be supervised, and they could receive support and encouragement from colleagues who were also committed to the idea of community involvement. This proved to work well.

Flexible, dynamic leadership

'Personalities are very important to any project,' say the project staff. This is particularly true where a personality is so closely associated with a neighbourhood, as in this project.

The mentor

There is also a supportive hierarchy within Cambridge HA for a community development approach: Dr Pat Troop, Director of Public Health, has been committed to the project from the outset, and has now successfully fought to convert the project's funding from joint finance (from 1985) into mainstream health authority funding as a development of the work of the health promotion department.

Support has also been given by Ian Nicholl, former chair of the health authority, and Dr Suan Goh, Registrar in Community Medicine.

The project in 1990

In summer 1990, when the project was visited for this report, it was going through a fallow period. Rosemary Cox and Gail Findlay, who had both been with the project since it started, had left in 1989 to further their careers, and two new workers – Sarah Procter and Veronica Speirs – were finding their feet and beginning to renew the networks with the community that had been through a period of interruption, despite interim workers being in place to try and create a temporary 'bridge'.

'The change of personnel has been unsettling – it is like taking a one-year step back. Some people are grieving for the loss of the people whom they knew, and we in our turn have to renew people's faith in this project,' says Sarah Procter. There is a great deal of enthusiasm and commitment from the new team, and Rosemary Cox is to maintain an involvement with the project workers as a supervisor.

An advisory group has been set up with the City Council community development staff from the two neighbourhoods and the managers of both the City Council and the health authority staff.

The work of the project

1. East Barnwell

The East Barnwell neighbourhood has a population of approximately 6000 and the majority of the people who live there (though not all) are registered at the East Barnwell Health Centre, which is known for developing a number of innovative health promotion initiatives. This progressive practice also has a Practice Participation Association, founded in 1983, which is an association of professionals and people registered with the practice. There is also a regular newsletter, which goes to all patients registered with the practice.

Through the various networks within East Barnwell (newsletters, for example), a number of initiatives were set up:

- voluntary visiting scheme for the elderly
- women's health group
- Barnwell Crèche Project
- swimming action group
- community car scheme
- Ditton Fields Nursery School Parents' Drop-in
- women and depression group
- 8–12s after-school club
- Priory School Health Self-help Group
- Look After Yourself exercise group
- asthma self-help group
- mothers' relaxation group
- mother and toddler group.

The swimming action group is a key example of the type of support offered by the project. 'It is working in a completely different way. Your role is to activate and motivate people to take action themselves and not to do things for them. It's so easy when you have got professional training to be doing things *for* people when all the time you've got to keep reminding yourself "no, I'm not the person to do it – I've got to help people to do what *they* want to do" – so it's a sort of facilitating role.' (Gail Findlay, *Health is Catching* video)[2]

This group grew out of a meeting organised by the PPA where a consultant rheumatologist spoke about the problems of arthritis. In discussion afterwards, the subject of swimming came up, and in particular the problems of access/lack of facilities for the disabled at local swimming pools.

With the encouragement and help of the community health project worker, one woman, who was disabled with arthritis, decided to write about this issue in community newsletters and in the practice newsletter. She invited others who were interested to contact her – a group was born to begin further action, which included lobbying the council's amenities and recreation department. It was not always an easy ride: 'I didn't honestly think I would have kept it up, because there were times when I sent letters out and I didn't get any replies whatsoever, and I must admit I felt a bit disheartened . . . but she [the project worker] just kept . . . advising me . . . or giving me different ideas about how to go about it.' (Mrs V. Cullum, Swimming Action Group, quoted in *Health is Catching*)[2]

Finally, success became evident. A meeting between the group and the manager of the local swimming pool achieved a number of results, including special swimming sessions, priority parking, and help from pool attendants. The group's confidence enabled them to become actively involved in providing input at the planning stage in the building of another local swimming pool. The warmth and success of this group has spawned others, as members have met around other specific areas of interest.

2. King's Hedges

King's Hedges is a very different area from East Barnwell.

The review notes 'In King's Hedges she [the project worker] has no direct or official link with health professionals or GP practices in the area.' There is one GP practice based on Arbury Road, but the primary health care team attached to it is based half a mile away. As many people in the area go to a number of different GPs, there are a number of different health visitors and district nurses working with people living in the area – an obstacle to efficient networking and passing on of information.

A key development was the acquisition of the community house at 37 Lawrence Way, providing a meeting place for people. 'The women who come to Lawrence Way are predominantly no-car ladies – they have pushchairs and will travel – but travelling to town for themselves to get this kind of help is bottom of their list.' (Brenda Smith, women's counsellor, quoted in *Health is Catching*)[2]

Lawrence Way has also meant that day-to-day liaison has become closer with the other statutory agencies who share the same base. The health authority boundary of King's Hedges – like East Barnwell – is coterminous with the City ward, making overlap with council workers easier to achieve.

The following are examples of the networks built up in King's Hedges:

- residents' association – elderly support group
- women's health group, including issues such as cervical screening, assertiveness
- exercise group
- 'Tuesday Teashop' Group
- Wardens' support group.

'The project's main impact', as seen by Eileen Wall, health visitor, King's Hedges, 'has possibly been raising awareness of "health" in its broad sense amongst other workers, and improving working relationships between the various professionals working in the area, e.g. health workers, social workers, housing officers.' (quoted in *Community Development Health Project: a Review of Achievements So Far*[1])

The future

With new project workers now in place there will be a renewed impetus, and the health promotion and AIDS services are keen to see the project develop further – perhaps into other parts of the district, particularly the rural areas in the Fens around Cambridge.

References

1. Cambridge Health Authority *Community Development Health Project: a Review of Achievements So Far*. 1990.
2. Video and project report *Health is Catching*, available, price £19.95, from Cheryl Arnold, The Shed, Addenbrooke's, Cambridge.

Contact: Sarah Procter and Veronica Speirs
               Cambridge Health Promotion Service
               The Shed
               Addenbrooke's
               Hills Road
               Cambridge CB2 2QQ
               Tel: 0223 26686

The Albany Health Project 'Health Wise' Market Stall

The partners

Voluntary sector: Albany Health Project
Statutory sector: health visitors from the Waldron Health Centre, Deptford

'The Albany Project is all about people maintaining good health – both physically and socially, and we are also concerned about people's environment and their health and safety. The market stall has brought us together with local health visitors, and it has helped us to build a real relationship with them' (Albany Health project workers, 1990)

Background

The Albany Social Action and Community Centre is part of Deptford, in South-east London's docklands area. The community centre is a large, purpose-built building, and a thriving social meeting place for the local community as well as people from neighbouring Greenwich, Lewisham and Southwark. It is heavily used both during the week and at weekends. There is a mix of social and recreational facilities – cafeteria, crèches, and a number of small units to serve community needs: housing advice drop-ins, advice and help with employment, young people's projects, and the Albany Empire, a club/theatre. Notice boards burst with facilities to meet a wide variety of alternative health interests: acupuncture and homoeopathy are just some of the alternative therapies on offer.

The Albany Health Project is one of the key parts of the centre. Housed in one of the main corner units, it is recognisable by the sign hanging outside, and is open to the public, from 10.00 to 4.00 Monday to Friday, for information and advice. It was originally set up in 1977, 'to foster the health of the people of the area and not to service needs of individuals when they are sick', and

- to develop an understanding of health as a local issue which affects the whole neighbourhood
- to help residents organise a local response to some of those health needs not effectively covered by the NHS, for example preventive care
- to provide information and training for local residents in community work around health issues
- to aid communication between residents and the agencies that control resources and make policy decisions about health matters
- to support local NHS employees in their response to health needs in Deptford
- to evaluate the contribution of community workers in dealing with health as a community issue.

Funding

'Funding is always precarious,' say the project workers. The project limps along currently on support from the Albany Centre, and from the local authority, who pay the two part-time staff (each in theory working for 21 hours per week – but in practice often working more).

Funding for the market stall comes from the centre's own budget, and apart from leaflets from the local health promotion unit, their attitude is very much one of having to 'make do and mend', borrowing equipment needed, and producing their own materials. 'We can't afford printed balloons, so we hand-letter our own,' says Cathy Collymore. The Albany Project applied for general funding from the Look After Your Heart community project scheme, but was turned down. Now both the project staff and the health visitors are keen to try again to gain a grant for the market stall, and they plan to submit a joint application.

Activities

The Albany Health Project 'Health Wise' market stall is a successful partnership between the project and health visitors at the Waldron Health Centre. The health visitors are based here, on the Albany 'patch', and five minutes' walk away from the centre. The stall started in 1988, after members of the Albany visited the Bethnal Green Health Project, who were using a market stall to give information to the public. In discussion with local health visitors it emerged that one of the health visitors had also been involved in running a stall in Brixton market, and the idea of running a local market stall was born.

Although the project wanted a covered stall in the market, there were insufficient funds, and an out-door stall was set up instead. Held on alternate Wednesdays in Deptford Market, the stall is serviced by a team consisting of one of the project's two workers, and two health visitors (provided on a rota basis which includes the school nurses or district nurses). Deptford Market is the biggest street market in the area, stretching from the High Street to Douglas Way, and taking place twice a week, drawing people from all over South London. It was chosen as an ideal focus to go out and talk to the community about health issues.

A different health issue is the central focus each time on the stall. Topics are decided several months in advance, when a joint planning meeting is held between the project staff and the health visitors. Topics have included: school health (which also involved the school nurse); alternative health care; foot health, stress-related illnesses, hypothermia, as well as support for national health education initiatives such as National Drinkwise Day and National No Smoking Day. Printed health education material – from either the local health promotion unit, or produced by the Health Project – is available on the stall to act as a support, with 'crowd-drawing' ideas such as hand-drawn balloons with appropriate health messages on to give away to children. An average market day sees people visiting the stall for advice either on the topic of the day, or for a chat on other health issues.

As well as the market staff, the project runs a number of health-related sessions throughout the week:

- women's health group: a chance for women to get together each week to discuss health issues of interest to them and provide mutual support
- acupuncture: offered at the project on an appointment basis for local people. A small fee to cover basic costs is charged
- ante-natal group: this group is run by an independent midwife, and gives women the chance to share experiences and ideas, to learn more about their pregnancy, giving birth and coping with a new baby
- post-natal group: held in the Albany Centre's crèche, this group provides a chance for new mothers to meet informally, to share information and support.

The Albany's mother and baby groups see some mothers who do not want to be visited by health visitors. This is a point of difficulty for the project – these mothers are their clients, and if they are not keen to see health professionals, the project does not want to push them towards them. 'If mothers do not want to have their babies immunised, then we believe that's their choice, even though it may not be the advice a health visitor would give them. Instead, we try to give them information and empower them to make that choice for themselves, and to make it a well-informed decision,' comments Monica Coombes.

- panic and anxiety group: a self-help group for people suffering from anxiety and stress-related problems, for example tranquilliser withdrawal, agoraphobia and panic attacks
- massage group: run in 1990, it helped people to see the benefits of relaxation and the therapeutic value of massage. It also aimed to teach the technique of massage. In its place, a new group on eating disorders will start up in 1991
- relationship support group. A women-only group which deals with relationship problems and aims to offer support and understanding
- Latin American women's health group: meets on alternative weeks and gives women from the Spanish-speaking community the opportunity to come together to share experiences and learn about all aspects of health
- 'Healthy Eating' classes: the unit has several rooms and a well-equipped kitchen where the cookery classes are run weekly, both for interested members of the public and for students with specific learning difficulties from the local adult education centre. The project is particularly proud of this initiative which has led to several of the students taking up work in the catering profession
- complementary medicine: there is a thriving demand within the Albany Centre for alternative therapies – many groups advertise their meetings and lectures, and they recently ran a six-week course on complementary medicine, which attracted a large attendance.

Evaluation

Although evaluation was not built in at the start of the 'Health Wise' stall project, both sides regard it as important to keep statistics, both of the number of people who approach the stall, and of the sort of questions that are asked. The health visitors, in particular, were keen to have this information to assure their own managers that their time was being used cost-efffectively. But health visitors have noticed other factors. 'Most of us enjoy it because it is a very different pace of working. Although we are meeting a lot of our own clients, we feel we are reaching other members of the community as well, and it shows them that we can talk to them about something other than potty training and feeding,' says Stephanie, one of the health visitors. 'We believe it's part of the health visitor role to be seen around the community, and to get involved, as needs are changing within the scope of the role of the health visitor.'

Evaluation of the Albany Project's work is being done by the Albany Centre, as part of an examination of its own work.

Working together – mutual respect and credibility with professionals

'It's taken several years to get this co-operation going, and it's been hard work. At the beginning the project took a lead, and then the health visitors joined in. Although we've not always seen eye to eye, we have learnt to value working with them, and we've also learned that health visitors are human and not as rigid as we thought they were! And we have a better working relationship because we are working in partnership on a project,' say the project workers.

The Albany Health Project's involvement with health visitors on the market stall has presented another way in which health visitors can work, apart from their accepted traditional role of visiting parents at home. Health visitors see more of the work that the project does; many drop in to the classes. The stall has provided a valuable 'bridge' between the project and part of the local primary care team, though the project, ideally, would like to build a similar link with local GPs, whom they have traditionally found hard to reach. 'We see ourselves as complementing the Health Service locally. Perhaps GPs just "tolerate" us, on the basis that we are not doing any harm, and anyway they feel it's not "real" health work,' say the project workers. Cathy and Monica would welcome a relationship with local GPs where specific tasks were delegated to the project.

Contact: Cathy Collymore and Monica Coombes
          Albany Health Project
          The Albany Centre
          Douglas Way
          London SE8 4AG
          Tel: 081-692 0231

PARTNERSHIPS GIVING HELP AND ADVICE

WHERE - Wellington Health Education Resource Enterprise

Health Information

'We feel we are creating a model health and information service to promote positive health, which has strong co-operative links with all local voluntary, self-help and statutory bodies. But in carrying out our work we have come to realise more and more that there is not just one simple straightforward and precise definition of the word "health". What we have begun to realise is that we have to be flexible in dealing with people's "health" problems and "take our brains for a walk" in attempting to find solutions' – Harry Clark Wilson, October 1990

Background

Wellington is a small Somerset town of around 12 000 people, with a traditionally caring and supportive community spirit. Set in the picturesque rural South-West, the area has a high proportion of older people, many of whom have moved to the South-West to retire, away from their immediate family. This lack of extended family is a common problem with modern society. WHERE attempts to address this as well as other common problems, including stress, disadvantage and unemployment.

The mentor

In 1988 Dr Bernard Newmarch, a local GP, perceived a need for a community-based service that would complement the activities of the general practitioners in the area, and would encourage 'people to participate individually and collectively in their own health care', as foreseen by the World Health Organisation. With his enthusiasm and commitment – and the support from the eleven other GPs in the area, the concept of WHERE was born, and a management committee created. WHERE is now a registered charity, Dr Newmarch is chair of the management committee, and his support is invaluable. As Harry Clark Wilson, the director, points out, it is not just of value with other health professionals, but with commercial companies – letters signed by a doctor add credibility and kudos to fund-raising efforts.

Flexible dynamic leadership

Early in 1989 Harry Clark-Wilson was appointed on half-time salary as director, with a brief to do three things: to find premises, to raise funds and to set up WHERE's administrative base. This half-time post (supported by a team of six volunteers) has become a full-time commitment, generating more and more work, particularly in the pressing quest to find funds. WHERE uses whatever volunteer help it can, offering every flexibility to staff – for example, one disabled volunteer works from home, researching and writing material for WHERE's own series of publications.

Activities

WHERE is an information source, rather than an advice point. It provides:

- up-to-date information on health matters presented in an easily understandable way (including producing, in consultation with local GPs, some of its own material, such as leaflets on 'Adolescence', 'The Menopause', etc.
- information on where further help can be obtained
- a free and confidential service
- a focal point for other community support services, for example Citizens Advice Bureau, Volunteer Bureau.

WHERE tried without success to obtain reasonably-priced shop premises, and has settled instead for a portakabin, purchased from a local CAB. The site it occupies – in a large car park in Wellington's Fore Street – is rented from the local authority, and WHERE's display board clearly signposts the entrance to passers-by. As well as displaying over 1000 leaflets on health-related subjects, the portakabin offers access to a computerised database with the names of over 100 other agencies in Wellington itself, each with their own specific expertise, together with nation-wide self-help and support groups currently totally a further 600 listings.

WHERE has several aims: 'Nowadays', says Harry Clark-Wilson, 'there is a constant flow of official information, which frequently changes, due to transient issues and media interpretation and presentation. This can create anxiety for many, especially older people, the disabled and socially disadvantaged. The aim of WHERE is to establish a focal point for information which reduces time, effort, stress and cost for members of the public in times of need.'

Secondly, WHERE acts as a networking link to enable all members of the community to have easy access to other organisations. Finally, it offers confidential counselling on a range of problems that are health-related in the broadest sense, because emotional problems are often the precursor to health problems.

The portakabin also provides accommodation for a number of other agencies to run 'clinics':

- the local Citizens Advice Bureau, which provides its usual range of advice and information
- the Wellington Volunteer Bureau, which holds two sessions a week and places volunteers with local groups. WHERE encourages clients to consider volunteering and considers that many people have actively found new interests as volunteers
- health visitors, who are available to answer questions on general health matters. The health visitors have also run special sessions where groups of schoolchildren visit the portakabin, to talk about subjects such as 'what happens when you go into hospital'
- social workers, who provide advice particularly for older people and those with physical difficulties or mental health problems.

Skills and credibility with other professionals

WHERE enjoys considerable support from health professionals locally. WHERE's management committee includes a local GP, a health visitor, the librarian, representatives from the County Council's Community Education Department, the local Volunteer Bureau, the Citizens Advice Bureau, the Probation Service, the County Council's Social Services Department, the Taunton Deane Council for Voluntary Service and the health authority.

A measure of the organisation's credibility is that many clients come on the suggestion of their GP, who will frequently suggest that a patient follows up a visit to the surgery with a visit to WHERE. And while consultations are confidential, there is good two-way communication, between the Wellington GPs and WHERE staff.

'Research shows that only 20 per cent of patients initially use the services of a doctor as a first resource in dealing with health problems, often preferring to obtain information from a friend, a member of the family or a chemist. It is also true to say that having consulted a doctor, patients are often shocked and possibly confused and anxious or stressed by what they have been told,' says Harry Clark-Wilson.

Funding

Funding comes at present via Joint Consultative Committee finance from the local authority and the health authority (an example of the difficulty in separating out the health and social issues involved), with a grant of £600 from the District Health Authority. Somerset County Council's Community Education department this year provided £3500. Other smaller amounts are energetically raised: by tackling local companies, by jumble sales on stalls outside the car park, and from sponsored events at local pubs. WHERE experiences the all-too-common problems of lurching on from year to year without secure core funding, with the knowledge that the present funders are all having their own budgets cut back.

Businesslike approach

WHERE is very conscious of the need to adopt a businesslike approach. It is keen to develop and sell its services, and is hoping to conduct research on prospective products and purchasers. Harry Clark-Wilson is hopeful that a link developed with the nearby town of Street may also lead to another WHERE offshoot being created in that town, and interest is being shown by voluntary organisations in other districts.

Evaluation

Evaluation of WHERE's work was introduced at the beginning of the project, with reseaerch being carried out among GPs, health professionals, together with community workers, teachers, the clergy, voluntary organisations, etc. on the sort of service they wanted. A sample of the general public was also approached (via an on-street survey) and asked what services they thought were needed. Calls and visits to the portakabin are logged; in just over a year WHERE has dealt with over 700 queries. Clients are asked to feed back information to the project, and to let the organisation know whether their help has been useful, or where shortcuts could be developed. 'We value very much the positive reports we get,' says Harry.

The future

A number of new projects are currently under way including: a teaching package entitled 'Why the need for an information service like WHERE?' Together with slides, this has been presented in the form of a lecture to doctors at the local postgraduate centre, as well as to voluntary, self-help and other charitable groups; and an 'attracting opposites' scheme, which aims to encourage schoolchildren to do voluntary work in conjunction with old people's clubs. However, the main aim is to provide a better, growing service: 'We will continue to work on updating, expanding, evaluating and improving the service provided for the public. Our long-term objective is to open further Health Information Bureaux in other towns in order to fulfil a perceived need.'

Contact: Harry Clark-Wilson
          Director
          WHERE (Wellington Health Education Resource Enterprise)
          The Portakabin
          Fore Street Car Park
          Wellington, Somerset
          Tel: 0823 665896

Preston Health Promotion Unit Media Project with Red Rose Radio

RED ROSE RADIO

The partners

Statutory sector: Preston Health Promotion Unit in association with Blackpool Health Promotion Unit
Voluntary sector: Action Desk (Community Service Volunteers)
Other: Red Rose Radio (independent station)

'Health professionals are generally cynical about media coverage of health issues. We believe that radio is sympathetic to the aims and objectives of health promotion, and we combine high profile media coverage with a community development approach, doing good public education in an innovative way' – Dominic Harrison (Preston Health Promotion Unit) and Action Desk team

Background

Red Rose Radio's Action Desk was set up in 1986, and was originally funded by the government's Community Programme Scheme to provide training for the unemployed.

Within the current partnership, each partner has distinct roles to play. Preston Health Promotion Unit secures funding, provides advice on health issues and contacts within the health professionals' network. The work is seen very much as part of the HPU's 'mission statement':

- to improve the level of good health of the people of Preston
- to reduce the dependence of the people of Preston on hospitals, medical and social services.

Community Service Volunteers provides what is currently a seven-member team servicing the Action Desk, and Red Rose Radio, a commercial station with a listenership of about half a million people, servicing Preston and the surrounding area. The unit broadcasts on Red Rose Gold AM at 12.30 pm daily (Monday to Friday) for about four minutes each day, and on Rock FM 4 times a day (approximately one minute each time) at 10.45 am, 2.45 pm, 7.45 pm, and 10.45 pm, Monday to Friday.

Split into AM and FM stations, Red Rose is a popular station with an audience rating fast approaching those of BBC Radios One and Two for its respective services. Possibly the only disadvantage for the project is that as it is firmly seen as an offshoot of Red Rose Radio, local newspapers are reluctant to give coverage to what is seen as the campaigns and issues of a competitor.

Action Desk is committed to 'social action' broadcasting. Its aims are:

- to provide information and advice to the general public through on-air broadcasting and off-air back-up
- to empower individuals
- to act as a bridge to voluntary agencies
- to encourage 'programme development', i.e. not treating issues as a one-off event
- to reflect local needs and to work in partnership
- to raise the profile of a local issue and put it on the public agenda
- to act as a referral agency.

In 1988 the Action Desk as it then was developed links with Preston's Health Promotion Unit, and began to look at ways in which radio could be used to broadcast health promotion messages. It came up with a package of activities for the Look After Your Heart campaign – a combination of broadcasting from a local shopping centre; an off-air phone-in; and programmes on air. The success of this persuaded the Regional Health Authority to provide £13 000 to fund a health promotion project at Red Rose Radio, with a dedicated project worker, working across Blackpool and Preston Health Districts.

Activities

The work of Action Desk is currently involved split into two main areas:

1. Health issues

Action Desk and the HPU drew up a list of the range of different health issues they want to tackle each month. In 1989, these included: January: Bodycare; February: Women's health matters – cervical smear testing; March: National No Smoking Day campaign.

Initially, a follow-up pack of health information was developed to support a range of topics. This evolved into a monthly magazine, of which 1000–2000 copies are available, sent free to anyone who phones in to Action Desk to request one. They are also available free to callers at Red Rose Radio's reception.

Occasionally, one-off booklets are produced on other topics, for example, *Radiation*, *Health Hazards at Work*, *Carers' Handbook* and *Women and Exercise*. Booklets and other material are always produced to a very high standard, and the team has its own graphic artist. Support for this project not only involves Dominic Harrison from the Health Promotion Unit, but a colleague from neighbouring Blackpool Health Promotion Unit.

The project has run a Health Line with the help of two local doctors who gave time to run a confidential off-air phone-in. Discussions are now under way with local GPs on the possibility of producing a patient education pack, guided by the FHSA – to educate and inform patients on what they can expect from their doctor.

2. *HIV/AIDS project*

This project is part of the HEA's Community Youth Project, which is a two-year project concerned with the preparation of young people as peer group educators. It is part of the HEA's HIV/AIDS and Sexual Health Programme's strategy to reach young people in informal community settings.

A special project worker at Action Desk works with groups of young people to discuss the issues surrounding AIDS and to explore ways of developing those issues into topics that can be approached in a specific magazine, to be distributed through youth networks. *Studio One* appears several times a year, and is made available through youth clubs and libraries. The project worker is also planning to develop live radio broadcasts by youth groups.

Funding

The Health Project is funded by Preston Health Promotion Unit and the Regional Health Authority (although it is subsidised at present by Action Desk). The media/aids worker post is funded by the HEA, and there is one other project worker who is funded by the minority ethnic funding section of the HEA. Funding – although reasonably secure – is short-term and is geared to projects. It is also paid in arrears. 'We need five-year core funding – but most of all we need "up-front" funding – we cannot work on deficit budgets and we cannot get lending facilities from banks to help us,' say Action Desk.

The mentor and hierarchical support

The project has been championed not only by the HPU but by senior staff at the Regional and District Health Authorities, 'and it has sometimes been a case of painful negotiation to match particular agendas,' says Dominic Harrison.

However, involvement of the media is seen as a great bonus in helping to remind the health authority of the value of the project: 'We have been able to show senior staff how radio can work for them. One particular example is when the Director of Public Health interviewed Edwina Currie on radio for us.'

Mutual respect

The HPU is situated a mile from Action Desk – but there is still a team feeling. It is a partnership where three different cultures work together: the infrastructure of the health authority combining with the sales-oriented approach of Red Rose, and the social action broadcasting approach of CSV.

There is also a great deal of inter-agency trust: often, Action Desk can be dealing with sensitive issues, for example under-age sex. The Action Desk team are aware of the sensitivity of broadcasting and publishing such material, and they aim to produce material that is not only highly professional, but sensitively geared – so as to be appropriate, but not antagonise or cause offence. 'Both the Health Promotion Unit and Red Rose trust us – there is never any checking of material by them prior to broadcast or publication,' say the team, 'mainly because we are very well aware of the need for thorough research and careful handling of very sensitive issues.'

Flexible, dynamic leadership

Deadlines – as in most media – rule the relationship; it is a fast-acting set-up, with deadlines for copy for magazines and leaflets which must be ready in time for broadcasts; and phone lines needing to be manned.

Businesslike approach

Action Desk is well equipped to produce its material, with desk-top publishing and offices in the centre of town, adjacent to the radio station. They would like to add cameras and video equipment, and expand the DTP system.

Evaluation

The project evaluates its work through regular reports. The May 1990 report included statistics of all publications and take-up rates. Lancaster University has also been involved in evaluating particular initiatives, for example the Drinkwise Day 1989 Campaign. The HIV/AIDS worker's post is the subject of a separate evaluation by Manchester University, which is being funded by the HEA as part of the cost of the project.

Contact: Nick College
Red Rose Radio Action Desk
1 Charnley Street
Preston
Lancs PR1 2UR
Tel: 0772 50903

or Dominic Harrison
Preston Health Promotion Unit
Preston Health Authority
Watling Street Road
Fulwood
Preston
Lancs PR2 4DX
Tel: 0772 711215

PARTNERSHIPS WITH EMPHASIS ON PROVIDING NEW NHS FACILITIES

Mike Heaffey Sports and Rehabilitation Centre, Stanmore, Middx

ASPIRE

The partners

Voluntary sector:	ASPIRE, Association for Spinal Injury, Research Rehabilitation and Reintegration
Statutory sector:	North East Thames Regional Health Authority
	North West Thames Regional Health Authority
	Bloomsbury Health Authority
	Management of Royal National Orthopaedic Hospital
Other partners:	The Sports Council
	Harrow Leisure Services

Background

ASPIRE was set up in 1983 by a group of concerned individuals to support the London Spinal Unit in its work. Through the voluntary group's dynamic fund-raising efforts, over £2m was raised to build and equip the purpose-built centre and sports hall, which have direct wheelchair access from the Spinal Injuries Unit at the hospital. The centre follows RNOH's philosophy of getting spinal injury victims up and about as soon as possible after an accident, with an aggressive-sounding programme that aims for independence from day one.

At the time when ASPIRE decided to build the centre, the RNOH was housed principally in hutted wards on sloping grounds in the leafy hills of Stanmore. Patients in wheelchairs were dependent on porters to push them to the rehabilitation unit where they underwent physiotherapy and occupational therapy. 'Finally', says Shannie Ross, honorary secretary of ASPIRE, 'we knew that if we wanted to give patients a better quality of life, we, rather than the health authority, would have to make the running.'

ASPIRE surveyed other disabled groups to find out whether they too would use the centre, if it were built, and what facilities they would want from it. Input from the London Borough of Harrow and the Sports Council helped ensure that all possible criteria were taken into account that would make the sports facilities second to none – there are, for example, four badminton courts rather than two, and an international-sized basketball court. Andrew Walker, the architect, is an ex-patient of the London Spinal Unit, injured when he fell through a rooflight. His aspirations for the centre were that it should be light, airy and modern – and all courts, all toilets and all facilities are designed to be used and enjoyed by people in wheelchairs.

The history of the project has not been without its clashes and its ups and downs. Bloomsbury Health Authority acted as client for the project and as such attended all project meetings, together with representatives from Harrow Leisure Services, the Sports Council, the hospital management, consultants and paramedics, the building consultants, etc. 'Because of all this input the project grew in size and cost over the project meetings stage – what had started life as a £400 000 project grew into a £1.3 million one!', says Shannie Ross. She continues: 'North East Thames Regional Health Authority's lay members as well as its officers were kept fully informed of the project and its progress. However, building consultants retained, the project having been put out to tender, the contractor selected and ASPIRE having paid approximately £150 000 to Bloomsbury Health Authority to bring the project to this stage, ASPIRE received its first communication from Sir David Berriman, the Chairman of the Region, advising them to halt the project as the Regional Health Authority wished to investigate the possibility of relocating the RNOH to Chase Farm Hospital in Enfield.'

'At that time ASPIRE had raised the £1.3 million necessary as well as having a £300 000 sinking fund to supplement the running of the centre for a period of five years. A costly feasibility study was implemented by the health authority on the advisability of a move to Enfield, a document prepared and responded to by countless people and organisations during which time the Action Committee of the RNOH secured 110 000 signatures on a petition, the consultants produced their signatures on a document drawn up by Hugh Dykes, MP and ASPIRE was in correspondence with every Member of Parliament and many sympathetic peers,' recounts Shannie Ross.

This delay cost ASPIRE much heartache, culminating in bad press for both charity and health authority when a donation that had been made was demanded back with interest. 'We risked having to give everything back,' she adds.

Hugh Dykes, MP had secured over 150 signatures on an Early Day Motion and an Adjournment Debate took place on 3 March 1988.

Finally, Sir David Berriman announced that ASPIRE could proceed with its plans to build the Mike Heaffey Centre and that the health authority or its successors would underwrite the re-provision of the facilities if in the future a move was necessary.

'Two years passed during which time building costs rose by £600 000. The Regional Health Authority made good the £30 000 donation ASPIRE had had to return but refused to make any further payment to ASPIRE despite the fact that its delaying tactics were to cost us over half a million pounds,' says Shannie Ross.

Further lobbying of MPs and peers, High-Churchmen and disability groups by ASPIRE resulted in a Parliamentary question being asked by Sir Geoffrey Finsberg, MBE JP MP, which was to produce £90 000 over two years from the North East and North West Regional Health Authorities.

Mutual respect, skills and credibility with other professionals

'Since that time, relationships have been very good between the health authorities and ourselves,' says Shannie Ross. 'We – a national charity – are based "on the premises" of RNOH, and we enjoy a wonderful relationship with health professionals here and at management levels in the health authorities.'

Businesslike approach

ASPIRE runs the centre as a limited company, with the aim, says Peter Sharkey, the centre manager, 'of running a commercial enterprise that aims to integrate the able-bodied and people with disabilities.' The spinal injury unit has first call on the sports facilities of the centre, but Peter's task is to offset the centre's running costs in the short term. In the longer term it is hoped to make the centre 'financially self-supporting'. He is currently involved in selling sessions at the centre to local schools, and, through Harrow Leisure Services involvement, it is included in the area's list of sports facilities.

The management committee of the centre is a partnership, between:

- the Sports Council
- Harrow Leisure Services
- RNOH administrative staff
- Peter Sharkey (centre manager)
- an ASPIRE trustee (medical).

The committee is chaired by the director of the centre, an ASPIRE committee member.

'It's a very business-orientated team which works well,' says Peter Sharkey. 'Everyone has been involved, and we have all pulled together.' ASPIRE feel that the commitment of the team, together with the professional approach which they have adopted – and which has been very much a hallmark of their management committee – has been the key factor that will guarantee success of the centre. It is probably fair to say that it is a centre dedicated to excellence, giving people that 'push' back into life, and using ingenuity and enterprise as a means to do it.

Evaluation

ASPIRE say that their problem in evaluating their work stems from how to measure the psychological benefit to patients from being able to direct themselves to such a unit. At present, they monitor use of all the sports facilities (with individual patient/user questionnaires periodically), and are considering what further evaluation they should attempt.

The future

The centre's pragmatic attitude towards business management means that they will be seeing how they can pull in more customers from the locality as well as finding more ways that people with disabilities and the able-bodied can take part in sports together.

'All we need now', believes Peter Sharkey 'is a slight deviation of bus route from the local bus companies, and we could offer all the facilities we have to more people.'

ASPIRE continues to fund-raise for other projects that will be carried out in partnership with health professionals, such as clinical trials on the electrical stimulation of paralysed muscles to improve health and mobility. They are also involved in the development, in conjunction with TV's 'Spitting Image' engineering company, of a powered, wheelchair-mounted manipulator arm.

The RNOH has applied for NHS Trust status. ASPIRE's lawyer is still attempting to finalise an agreement with Bloomsbury Health Authority concerning the responsibilities and liabilities of the centre.

Contact: Shannie Ross, MBE
Honorary Secretary
ASPIRE
Royal National Orthopaedic Hospital
Brockley Hill
Stanmore
Middx HA7 4LP
Tel: 081-954 0164

PARTNERSHIPS CREATING HEALTHY LIFESTYLES

The National Forum for Coronary Heart Disease Prevention - School Meals Assessment Project

'As a project, it fits so well with so many different areas. The balance between "local" and "national" works very well, too. There are lots of different interest groups involved, and we've recognised it could get fraught, but we've worked well together without being competitive.' (Imogen Sharp, National Forum for Coronary Heart Disease Prevention)

The partners

Voluntary sector: National Forum for Coronary Heart Disease Prevention
Statutory sector: Hampstead District Health Authority: Health Promotion Department
Polytechnic of North London: School of Life Sciences

Background

The School Meals Assessment project is a partnership between the National Forum for Coronary Heart Disease Prevention and Hampstead District Health Authority's Health Promotion Department.

The assessment programme developed from a workshop on coronary heart disease prevention in school-age children, held in October 1988. The aim was to develop a simple, universally-understandable method of assessing the nutritional standard of school meals, set against a background of the 1980 Education Act, that had removed the statutory nutritional standards for school meals.

The project – which is still being piloted and refined – aims to produce a method of assessment that is suitable for a wide range of users: parents, school governors, teachers, caterers, school nurses, as well as pupils. The assessment may indicate areas where the meals offered could be improved, and particularly highlight those areas contributing a large amount of fat. A diet of this kind in childhood has been implicated in the development of coronary heart disease.

How the School Meals Assessment Package works

At the moment the School Meals Assessment Package (SMAP) includes

121

introductory materials, food fact guidelines, and user guides to the two possible forms of assessment – a written and a computer method. Schools choose either the written or the computer method, based on their own requirements, the ability of the users, and the availability of a computer.

Both forms work on the same principle – the assessor describes the dishes on the menu by answering a series of multiple-choice questions.

Having described the dishes being assessed, the assessor is shown a nutritional breakdown, either at the press of a button on the computer version, or after some basic arithmetic in the written format.

The results are shown as figures, or columns on a histogram, illustrating the quantity of each nutrient present in the food being assessed. The recommended lunchtime intake for each nutrient is also shown, so it is possible to see clearly whether nutrients are inside or outside accepted NACNE and COMA guidelines.

The assessment packages will be accompanied by teaching material, with guidance on action that can be taken. The computer version already provides opportunities for modification to improve the 'healthiness' of the meals on offer – for example, using soft cooking fat instead of lard, liquid frying oils instead of solid, using a mixture of wholemeal and white flour rather than only white.

Because assessments are based on the information entered, it is important to have accurate data about the type of ingredients used – hard fats, white flour, sweetened fruit, etc. and the cooking methods. All of this must be obtained from the caterer, using the food fact guidelines, which provides a vital start to the project – a mechanism for ensuring communication between caterer and customer.

'School cooks, who have been invited to participate in the study, have a wealth of knowledge about what children will eat, but need the support of the whole school to implement changes towards the uptake of healthier choices,' says Imogen Sharp. 'SMAP is ideal in this situation for both pupil teaching and as a monitoring tool.'

SMAP is being piloted through the science, technology and health education components of the National Curriculum, helping children learn food choice skills that they can apply not only to school meals but to their wider eating habits. Using SMAP as a learning instrument has been the main thrust of the first stage of the pilot study in a number of secondary schools in Camden and in Brent. In these schools the project officer has worked with teachers to incorporate SMAP into a class programme over a series of lessons, either as a whole-class activity or as an individual project. The work involves pupils in examining NACNE and COMA guidelines, assessing their own foods in relation to those guidelines, and looking at ways of improving their food choices.

The project is an evolving process – the pilot study will produce information on refinements necessary to make the SMAP activities (and consequently the skills required) available to a wide range of users.

The next stage will be aimed at those responsible for school meals contracts and nutritional monitoring at school and LEA level.

Support for the project

Following the initial workshop in 1988, Dr Noel Olsen, who was honorary secretary of the National Forum for Coronary Heart Disease Prevention, and also Director of Public Health at Hampstead Health Authority, saw the potential for the project and supported it. He arranged for early meetings to be held to refine the ideas and to bring together a small team of interested parties, including Imogen Sharp, Coordinator of the National Forum and Sue Rodmell, Director of the Health Promotion Department in Hampstead. Maggie Sanderson, a lecturer at the Polytechnic of North London, who represents the British Dietetic Association on the National Forum, was also at this initial meeting. With her help, the project was able to obtain the services of a dietetics student who carried out a validation study – comparing portion sizes used in the assessment package against the real portion sizes served in schools.

A larger working group was then convened by Maggie Sanderson. This consisted of relevant member organisations of the National Forum, the National Association of School Meals Organisers, and ILEA. Although not involved in specific testing, this group provided expert guidance and consultation.

There was also a local dimension, which helped to ensure the involvement of people who might participate in the Hampstead pilot study. This included LEA catering staff, educationists and school nurses. The project has also been endorsed as an inter-sectoral initiative by the Camden Healthy Cities project, and will be used by other catering offices in Camden in the design of menus. (Case studies of the UK Health for All Network and Hull Healthy City Initiative appear earlier – see pp. 89–94.)

Funding

Funding for the pilot project to date has come from the Health Education Authority's Look After Your Heart programme. This has provided a budget for a project officer, Gill Cawdron, to be employed on a contract basis, to liaise with schools, school catering organisers, school caterers, teachers and pupils to assess the ease, relevance and opportunities of using SMAP. Evaluation has always been considered an integral part of the programme.

The future

The findings of the pilot study will contribute to refinement and improvement of the package as a whole, and in highlighting its various uses, particularly in the National Curriculum. 'We have more evaluation and re-piloting to do,' says Imogen Sharp. 'We are seeking funding for national dissemination, and we intend that the relevant member organisations of the National Forum will help with this, by giving credibility and access to their networks. The project has gone very smoothly so far because we feel it has had all the right ingredients, particularly a team of key individuals who work well together.'

Contact: Imogen Sharp
National Forum for Coronary Heart Disease Prevention
Hamilton House
Mabledon Place
London WC1H 9TX
Tel: 071-383 7638

Appendix 3 *EVALUATION – AN INTEGRAL PART OF THE PLANNING PROCESS*

Academics point to the fact that there has never been any long-term evaluation of health promotion. The evaluation exercises that have been carried out have all come from the educational field.

What is evaluation?

Evaluation is a way of justifying a project's existence, and of answering key questions about what it will achieve, such as:

'what will count as success?'
'what will count as showing we have failed to do what we set out to do?'
'how has the health of local communities been improved by our work?'
'what will demonstrate to current/potential funders that we deserve to have our funding renewed?'

Successful evaluations are never regarded as 'bolt-ons' to a project, but are considered at the very beginning of a project's existence, and continued as the project develops.

Why evaluate?

Reasons include the following:

- to monitor standards and quality
- to ensure relevance of service
- to explain to outsiders what the project is trying to achieve
- to monitor the process which the project undergoes
  Process evaluation is often referred to as a 'formative' evaluation and is distinguished from 'summative' or 'outcome' evaluation. Summative evaluation, as its name implies, 'sums up' a project and refers to outcomes or targets.
  Formative evaluation examines and documents what happens during the life of a project. It contains such things as the working practices, the feelings and attitudes of project members and consumers and it looks at these things in terms of how efficiently and effectively the project work is progressing. More than this, there is often a requirement of 'reflexibility' which gives constant feedback through the life of the project.
- to explain to outsiders what a project is trying to achieve
  With increased competition for funding, there is an increasing emphasis being placed on evaluation of projects. But there are benefits from evaluation – for instance, evaluation of Age Well Initiative in Eastbourne resulted in funding by Eastbourne HA of a permanent full-time Healthy Living Adviser.
  The problem is that the concept of 'value for money' is easier to

demonstrate where there are 'hard' tangible measurements involved, such as service delivery factors, numbers of people receiving information, or visiting a clinic.

If it's so essential, why don't people evaluate?

Among reasons put forward are the following:

- 'it means we'll have to be unduly negative or critical about people's performance' – in a sector which relies so heavily on goodwill of volunteers this is often seen as unduly threatening, whereas evaluation can either incorporate a self-generated evaluation, or be a useful opportunity for feedback from volunteers on the tasks they do
- 'we don't have the time' – some partnerships believe that spending time on evaluating is at the expense of 'getting on with the job'

This is borne out by a quote from one partnership: 'In the early stages of the project, we attempted, almost literally, to make evaluation "a continuous part of the dynamic process". For example, we kept comprehensive daily diaries of our work and also developed a "contact sheet" which recorded the nature and origin of daily contacts with individuals and groups in community and professional networks.

'It soon became clear that both the diary and the contact sheet were intrusive and unmanageable on a daily basis, and therefore not feasible over the whole period of the project. They were however in a sense very useful, though time-limited, tools, as they described the varied and unusual nature of networking and quickly began to amass the vast array of largely unpredictable factors and potential for different initiatives arising from the work.' (Cambridge Community Development Health Project: *Review of Achievements So Far*)

- 'we don't have the skills' – evaluation is seen as a specialist skill which most volunteers do not feel that they have
- 'how can we measure effectively the sort of qualitative service we provide?' – the biggest problem for health promotion projects – but there are 'softer', qualitative evaluation techniques that can be used, where the emphasis is on the more personalised, subjective view of customer satisfaction.

CHIC – the Chinese Health and Information Centre in Manchester, has produced an evaluation report of its work between 1987 and 1989. A combination of complementary methods have been developed for the evaluation of CHIC, including:

- routine data
- surveys
- non-participant observation
- group discussions with staff
- group discussion with users
- feedback questionnaires
- checklists

- professional assessment
- financial monitoring.

CHIC's report says: 'The different methods have difficulties and limitations, but in combination they help to give an overall picture. The methods are reviewed regularly by an evaluation subgroup of the steering committee, which includes the project co-ordinator, a general practitioner who works in the centre, a community physician and a research nurse employed part-time to carry out evaluation and development work.' (*Chinese Health and Information Centre Evaluation Report 1987–89*, CHIC, Manchester)

Partnerships should always attempt to evaluate what they do, seeking outside help if necessary, rather than simply dismiss the issues as being either irrelevant or in some way destructive of the ethos of volunteer help.

What sort of evaluation should be done?

'Any form of evaluation will be better than nothing at all . . . you *can* do away with all the philosophical and intellectual issues by reducing evaluation to a 'common-sense' process. Evaluation done well (however) is a very skilled job – not suitable for rank amateurs.' (Professional health evaluator's comment)

A detailed section on evaluation would be a book in itself, and there are already many extremely useful books available, for example see Institute of Health, Welfare and Community Education, *The Evaluation of Community Development Initiatives in Health Promotion: a Review of Current Strategies* (Open University Press, 1991). Organisations such as National Community Health Resource, and the Field Development Division of the HEA can refer partnerships to health promotion projects that have used evaluation as part of their way of working. Some health authorities have an evaluator on the staff (an example is Cambridge, who have an evaluator based in their health promotion unit).

Does evaluation mean extra work?

The short answer is inevitably Yes, but it is an investment that must be made to show that a project is working effectively and fulfilling its aims, and particularly vital if increased funding may be sought at a later stage.

As we have seen, the question of extra work is one of 'necessary evils' of evaluation which is most feared by partnerships involving voluntary organisations – they often simply do not have the 'slack' within their staffing to cope with complex evaluation, and even simple evaluation such as the keeping of records and diaries means an extra burden on staff time.

This factor makes it doubly necessary to consider evaluation at the outset of a project, so that when funding is being applied for, the costs of extra help with evaluation mechanisms (both in terms of extra time on those involved in the project) *and* in terms of possible extra help from outside, can be budgeted in.

Two possible methods of using outside help with evaluation are:

- the use of students

    Using students or a local university to help (as part of its coursework) can be a cost-effective way of obtaining specialised, postgraduate help on evaluation. If a local university or college is unable to help, the Research Department at the HEA may be able to provide help and guidance both on methods of evaluation they consider appropriate, and on how to find an appropriate source of student help.

- using other health professionals

    The Society of Health Education and Health Promotion Officers has established a professional audit and evaluation scheme, which they feel will offer valuable help to voluntary organisations wishing to carry out evaluation. 'We believe it is important that voluntary groups can call upon experienced field-level workers to conduct all their inner evaluation programmes for them, as in many cases we think this is much more appropriate than drafting in somebody from a university department who is unaware of many of the practical difficulties and realities faced by field-level health education/health promotion work,' says Jeff French, the society's secretary.

    The society's scheme offers auditors who have at least five years' experience at a senior level or above, together with a recognised postgraduate academic qualification. They are able to provide a written report and verbal feedback to whoever commissions the work.

    The audit 'is carried out against set principles defined by health education/promotion specialists, including the following key elements:

- client involvement in planning and evaluation
- the promotion of self-esteem and autonomy
- non-coercion and voluntarism
- sensitivity to social, economic and environmental factors influencing or of concern to clients
- the valuing of others
- the use of congruent evaluation
- responsibility for the accuracy of the information and the appropriateness of methods used for communication.'

    Each evaluation is separately costed. For further information contact: Jeff French, District Health Education Officer, the Society of Health Education and Health Promotion Officers, 11 Portland Square, Carlisle, Cumbria CA1 1PY (tel: 0228 515034).

    Finally, Charities Evaluation Services is a newly-formed charity, 'the main function of which will be to provide an evaluation advisory service for voluntary organisations'. Their literature also says that 'a primary objective of this service will be to equip voluntary workers with evaluation skills so that they are able to perform self-evaluation studies on behalf of their own organisations.' Charities Evaluation Services is at Forbes House, 9 Artillery Lane, London E1 7LP (tel: 071-377 2939).

Appendix 4 HEALTH FOR ALL IN EUROPE BY THE YEAR 2000: THE TARGETS

1   *Reducing the differences*

By the year 2000, the actual differences in health status between countries and between groups within countries should be reduced by at least 25 per cent, by improving the level of health of disadvantaged nations and groups.

2   *Developing health potential*

By the year 2000, people should have the basic opportunity to develop and use their health potential to live socially and economically fulfilling lives.

3   *Better opportunities for the disabled*

By the year 2000, disabled persons should have the physical, social and economic opportunities that allow at least for a socially and economically fulfilling and mentally creative life.

4   *Reducing disease and disability*

By the year 2000, the average number of years that people live free from major disease and disability should be increased by at least 10 per cent.

5   *Elimination of specific diseases*

By the year 2000, there should be no indigenous measles, poliomyelitis, neonatal tetanus, congenital rubella, diphtheria, congenital syphilis or indigenous malaria in the region.

6   *Life expectancy at birth*

By the year 2000, life expectancy at birth in the region should be 75 years.

7   *Infant mortality*

By the year 2000, infant mortality in the region should be less than 20 per 1000 live births.

8   *Maternal mortality*

By the year 2000, maternal mortality in the region should be less than 15 per 100 000 live births.

9   *Diseases of the circulation*

By the year 2000, mortality in the region from diseases of the circulatory system in people under 65 should be reduced by at least 15 per cent.

10   *Cancer*

By the year 2000, mortality in the region from cancer in people under 65 should be reduced by at least 15 per cent.

11   *Accidents*

By the year 2000, deaths from accidents in the region should be reduced by at least 25 per cent through an intensified effort to reduce traffic, home and occupational accidents.

12   *Suicide*

By the year 2000, the current rising trends in suicides and attempted suicides in the region should be reversed

13   *Healthy public policy*

By 1990, national policies in all member states should ensure that legislative, administrative and economic mechanisms provide broad intersectoral support and resources for the promotion of healthy lifestyles and ensure effective participation of the people at all levels of such policy-making.

14   *Social support systems*

By 1990, all member states should have specific programmes which enhance the major roles of the family and other social groups in developing and supporting healthy lifestyles.

15   *Knowledge and motivation for health behaviour*

By 1990, educational programmes in all member states should enhance the knowledge, motivation and skills of people to acquire and maintain health.

16   *Positive health behaviour*

By 1995, in all member states, there should be significant increases in positive health behaviour, such as balanced nutrition, non-smoking, appropriate physical activity and good stress management.

17   *Health-damaging behaviour*

By 1995, in all member states, there should be significant decreases in health-damaging behaviour, such as overuse of alcohol and pharmaceutical products; use of illicit drugs and dangerous chemical substances; and dangerous driving and violent social behaviour.

18   *Multisectoral policies*

By 1990, member states should have multisectoral policies that effectively protect the environment from health hazards, ensure community awareness and involvement, and support international efforts to curb such hazards affecting more than one country.

19   *Monitoring and control mechanisms*

By 1990, all member states should have adequate machinery for the monitoring, assessment and control of environmental hazards which pose a threat to human health, including potentially toxic chemicals, radiation, harmful consumer goods and biological agents.

20   *Control of water pollution*

By 1990, all people of the region should have adequate supplies of safe drinking-water and by the year 1995, pollution of rivers, lakes and seas should no longer pose a threat to human health.

21   *Control of air pollution*

By 1995, all people of the region should be effectively protected against recognised health risks from air pollution.

22   *Food safety*

By 1990, all member states should have significantly reduced health risks from food contamination and implemented measures to protect consumers from harmful additives.

23   *Control of hazardous wastes*

By 1995, all member states should have eliminated major known health risks associated with the disposal of hazardous wastes.

24   *Human settlements and housing*

By the year 2000, all people of the region should have a better opportunity of living in houses and settlements which provide a healthy and safe environment.

25   *Working environment*

By 1995, people of the region should be effectively protected against work-related health risks.

26   *A system based on primary health care*

By 1990, all member states through effective community representations, should have developed health care systems that are based on primary health care and supported by secondary and tertiary care as outlined at the Alma-Ata Conference.

27   *Rational and preferential distribution of resources*

By 1990, in all member states, the infrastructure of the delivery systems should be organised so that resources are distributed according to need and that services ensure physical and economic accessibility and cultural acceptability to the population.

28   *Content of primary health care*

By 1990, the primary health care system of all member states should provide a wide range of health-promotive, curative, rehabilitative and supportive services to meet the basic health needs of the population and give special attention to high-risk, vulnerable and underserved individuals and groups.

29   *Providers of primary health care*

By 1990, in all member states, primary health care systems should be based on co-operation and teamwork between health care personnel, individuals, families and community groups.

30   *Co-ordination of community resources*

By 1990, all member states should have mechanisms by which the services provided by all sectors relating to health are co-ordinated at the community level in a primary health care system.

31   *Ensuring quality of care*

By 1990, all member states should have built effective mechanisms for ensuring quality of patient care within their health care systems.

32   *Research strategies*

Before 1990, all member states should have formulated research strategies to stimulate investigations which improve the application and expansion of knowledge needed to support their Health for All developments.

33 *Policies for Health for All*

Before 1990, all member states should ensure that their health policies and strategies are in line with Health for All principles and that their legislation and regulations make their implementation effective in all sectors of society.

34 *Planning and resource allocation*

Before 1990, member states should have managerial processes for health development geared to the attainment of Health for All, actively involving communities and all sectors relevant to health and, accordingly, ensuring preferential allocation of resources to health development priorities.

35 *Health information systems*

Before 1990, member states should have health information systems capable of supporting their national strategies for Health for All.

36 *Planning, education and use of health personnel*

Before 1990, in all member states, the planning, training and use of health personnel should be in accordance with Health for All policies, with emphasis on the primary health care approach.

37 *Education of personnel in other sectors*

Before 1990, in all member states, education should provide personnel in sectors related to health with adequate information on the country's Health for All policies and programmes and their practical application to their own sectors.

38 *Appropriate health technology*

Before 1990, all member states should have established a formal mechanism for the systematic assessment of the appropriate use of health technologies and of their effectiveness, efficiency, safety and acceptability, as well as reflecting national health policies and economic restraints.

SOURCE: *Targets for Health for All: Targets in Support of the European Regional Strategy for Health for All* Copenhagen, WHO Regional Office for Europe, 1985 (European Health for All Series, No. 1).

Appendix 5 *QUESTIONNAIRE TO VOLUNTARY/ STATUTORY PARTNERSHIPS IN HEALTH PROMOTION*

26 Bedford Square,
London WC1B 3HU

Telephone: 071-636 4066

Facsimile: 071-436 3188

1 June 1990

Dear Colleague,

Voluntary/Statutory Partnerships in Health Promotion

The National Council for Voluntary Organisations is carrying out a project to identify the many health promotion projects in England that are being carried out by collaboration between a voluntary group and a statutory health provider. This is a six months project, funded by the Health Education Authority.

We are looking for details of all sorts of collaborative ventures in health promotion. These can be on a national, regional or local scale, and examples may vary from large voluntary bodies that are linked with health authorities or local authorities to provide a specific health promotion service, to small community ventures that involve a group of committed volunteers working directly with the local hospital, GP surgery or community nursing service. We are also keen to identify any projects that involve more than one partner - for example, other voluntary groups, other authorities, or even the commercial sector.

A number of projects will be visited in detail during the summer - and a report on the project will be published at the end of the year.

We would very much like to know whether your organisation is involved in - or supports - any such partnerships. A short questionnaire is enclosed, so that you can provide some details.

If you would like to send more information - or want to send it in a different form to the questionnaire - please feel free to do so. However, please note that the deadline for information is 30 June 1990.

If you have any queries about the project, would like more information, or wish to make any comments about this area, please contact Janet Hunter or Jenny Fieldgrass, at the address above.

Thank you in advance for all your help!

Yours sincerely

Jenny Fieldgrass
Project Worker

PROMOTING THE INTERESTS AND EFFECTIVENESS OF CHARITIES AND OTHER VOLUNTARY ORGANISATIONS.

Patron HM The Queen **President** Sir Kenneth Durham **Chair** Sir Geoffrey Chandler CBE **Vice-chairs** Barbara Hosking OBE and Kay Young OBE **Hon Treasurer** Geoffrey Foster **Director** Usha Prashar. A registered charity No. 225922. Company limited by guarantee. Registration No. 198344 England. Registered office as above

Questionnaire to voluntary/statutory partnerships in health promotion

26 Bedford Square,
London WC1B 3HU
Telephone: 071-636 4066
Facsimile: 071-436 3188

Joint National Council for Voluntary Organisations/Health Education Authority
Project on Voluntary/Statutory Partnerships in Health Promotion

Name of health promotion partnership/project

....

....

....

Co-ordinator's name/contact address ....

....

....

Please tell us who the partners are:

The voluntary sector partner is ....

....

who provides ....

....

....

....

The statutory sector partner is ....

....

who provides ....

....

....

....

If there are any other partners (e.g. commercial), please say who, and what they
provide

....

....

PROMOTING THE INTERESTS AND EFFECTIVENESS OF CHARITIES AND OTHER VOLUNTARY ORGANISATIONS.

Patron HM The Queen President Sir Kenneth Durham Chair Sir Geoffrey Chandler CBE Vice-chairs Barbara Hosking OBE and Kay Young OBE Hon Treasurer Geoffrey Foster
Director Usha Prashar. A registered charity No. 225922. Company limited by guarantee. Registration No. 198344 England. Registered office as above

135

Please tell us briefly what the partnership has achieved

....

....

....

....

(If the partnership produces any leaflets or other material please send us some examples)

Which health promotion areas does the project service? (e.g. women's health/ minority ethnic group health/AIDS/cancer)

....

Does the partnership carry out any activities in the workplace?

YES .... NO .... If YES, please give brief details

....

....

....

How long has the partnership been going? ....

How is the effectiveness of the partnership evaluated? ....

....

....

Please tell us about any positive attitudes the partnership has encountered

....

....

and about any obstacles the partnership has faced/how these have been overcome

....

....

....

This questionnaire completed by (name) ....

Organisation ....

Telephone number ....

Date ....

Appendix 6 *DIRECTORY OF ALL PARTNERSHIPS RESPONDING TO THE QUESTIONNAIRE*

Note

This directory was compiled from the questionnaires returned in 1990 for this report (with minor updating), and some changes in personnel or addresses may have taken place since then. Telephone numbers are given wherever possible.

Project Number 1	Language Line
	Language Line, 18 Victoria Park Square, Bethnal Green, London E2 9PF tel: 081-981 9911
Aims	To provide an interpreting service for Asian patients
Partners	Mutual Aid Centre/The London Hospital
Project Number 2	Joint Breastfeeding Initiative
	Alexander House, Oldham Terrace, London W3 6NH tel: 081-992 8637
Aims	To provide information and initiatives on breastfeeding and to encourage more mothers to consider breastfeeding as an option
Partners	NCT/La Leche League/Association of Breastfeeding Mothers/Department of Health
Project Number 3	Sheffield Afasic Regional Group Pre-school Project
	Association for all Speech-Impaired Children (AFASIC), 347 Central Markets, Smithfield, London EC1A 9NH tel: 071-236 3632
Aims	Education of young children with delayed language development with teaching strategies developed jointly by teachers and speech therapists
Partners	Speech therapists/language teachers/polytechnic lecturers
Project Number 4	East Yorkshire Health Authority training team for mental health work
	Mental Health Education Unit, East Yorkshire Health Authority, De la Pole Hospital, Willerby, Hull HU10 6ED
Aims	Assessing training needs and developing training programmes for all workers involved in mental health programmes
Partners	local voluntary organisations/Health Service staff (funding by health and social services departments)
Project Number 5	Blisslink Conference for Health Visitors (July 1990)
	Blisslink, 17–21 Emerald Street, London WC1N 3QL tel: 071-831 9393
Aims	Conference jointly organised by BLISSLINK and the HVA: 'Special Care Babies and their Families – Changing Perspectives in Care'
Partners	Voluntary organisations (Baby Life Support Systems/Stillbirth & Neonatal Death Association/Pre-school Playgroups Association/Nursery Nurses Association/ Health Visitors' Association)

Project Number 6	Maternity Links
	The Old Co-op, 38–42 Chelsea Road, Easton, Bristol BS5 6AF tel: 0272 558495
Aims	To provide support, understanding, information and interpreting to pregnant non-English-speaking women and their children using the Health Service
Partners	Bristol and Weston Health Authority/volunteers (including home tutors)
Project Number 7	Counselling service for families and patients attending limb lengthening clinic at Sheffield Children's Hospital
	Restricted Growth Association, c/o 61 Lady Walk, Maple Cross, Rickmansworth, Herts WD3 2YZ tel: 0923 770759
Aims	To give new patients individual counselling and to explore hopes and fears in undertaking this surgical procedure
Partners	Restricted Growth Association/Sheffield Children's Hospital
Project Number 8	Furness Cancer Support Group
	c/o 18 Maryport Avenue, Walney Island, Barrow in Furness, Cumbria LA14 3LR tel: 0229 41650
Aims	To provide support and drop-in centre for people with cancer
Partners	Partners: South Cumbria Health Authority/Macmillan Nursing Service/voluntary organisation (Furness Cancer Support Group)
Project Number 9	Mike Heaffey Sports and Rehabilitation Centre
	ASPIRE (Association for Spinal Injury, Research, Rehabilitation and Reintegration), Brockley Hill, Stanmore, Middlesex HA7 4LP tel: 081-954 0164
Aims	Building and running of sports centre for disabled and able-bodied people at Royal National Orthopaedic Hospital
Partners	ASPIRE/Royal National Orthopaedic Hospital/Regional Health Authority
Project Number 10	Midwifery Project for Bangladeshi Community
	c/o Tyne and Wear Racial Equality Council, 4th Floor, Mear House, Elephant Place, Newcastle upon Tyne NE1 8XS tel: 091-2327639
Aims	To meet Bangladeshi women and provide proper advice about pregnancy and childbirth
Partners	Tyne and Wear Racial Equality Council/Newcastle District Health Authority
Project Number 11	Wirral Women's Health Network
	c/o Women's Health Unit, Field Development Division, Health Education Authority, Hamilton House, Mabledon Place, London WC1H 9TX
Aims	To produce a video to show changing attitudes of partnerships with Health Service and voluntary organisations
Partners	60/70 voluntary organisations in Wirral area/Health Education Authority Women's Health Team Unit
Project Number 12	Glyndon Health Project
	106 Plumstead High Street, London SE18 1ST tel: 081-854 2966
Aims	To provide community initiatives on health
Partners	Local authority/health authority/voluntary organisations
Project Number 13	Skills for the Primary School Child
	c/o TACADE (The Advisory Council on Alcohol and Drug Education), 1 Hulme Place, The Crescent, Salford, Manchester M5 4QA
Aims	To provide a 'health skills' kit for primary-school children
Partners	Department of Education and Science/TACADE/RE-SOLV

Project Number 14	Chinese Health and Information Centre
	34 Princes Street, Manchester M1 4JP tel: 061-228 0138
Aims	To provide access to health services for the Chinese community
Partners	Chinese Health and Information Centre (charity)/District Health Authorities
Project Number 15	Plymouth Women's Health Fair (April 1990)
Aims	To run a women's health fair (this was the fourth fair to be staged in the south-west, but the first to include seminars and the first undertaken by Plymouth Health Authority)
Partners	Devon Family Practitioner Committee/Plymouth Community Health Council, plus numerous voluntary organisations
Project Number 16	Joint Planning on Mental Health in North-West Derbyshire
	Community Mental Health Team, 113 Dale Road, Matlock, Derbyshire DE4 3LU
Aims	To develop a community-orientated mental health service
Partners	Health authority/Social Services/local mental self-help groups/Council for Voluntary Service/other voluntary organisations such as Samaritans
Project Number 17	Chiltern Volunteer Bureau, Wycombe Volunteer Focus
	The Malt House, Elgiva Lane, Chesham, Bucks HP5 2JD tel: 0494 776156
Aims	To offer training courses for health care professionals and voluntary workers involved in the care of the terminally ill
Partners	Chiltern Volunteer Bureau, Wycombe Health Authority/Wycombe Volunteer Focus
Project Number 18	CADD (Campaign against Drinking and Driving)
	c/o Ringsmere Orchard, Pershore Road, Little Comberton, Pershore WR10 3HF tel: 038 674426
Aims	To promote a campaign against drinking and driving
Partners	CADD/Department of Transport
Project Number 19	Walsall Mastectomy and Breast Cancer Self-help Group
	c/o 11 Wharwell Lane, Great Wyrley, Walsall, West Midlands WS6 6ET tel: 0922 412731
Aims	Support group for mastectomy patients/fund-raising for dedicated chemotherapy unit at local hospital
Partners	Walsall Mastectomy and Breast Cancer Self-help Group/Walsall Manor Hospital
Project Number 20	The Food Chain
	100 Shepherdess Walk, London N1 7JN tel: 071-250 1391
Aims	To provide a service delivering healthy meals to patients with HIV-related illnesses at home in the London area
Partners	Volunteers/various Social Services departments/hospital dietitians in London boroughs
Project Number 21	Tunbridge Wells Cancer Centre
	c/o 48 Grosvenor Road, Tunbridge Wells, Kent TN1 2AB tel: 0892 541343
Aims	To work informally with nurses at local hospital. To take a holistic approach and provide treatment that is complementary to the orthodox medical treatment provided by the hospital
Partners	Volunteers/nurses at Pembury Hospital
Project Number 22	Hounslow and Whitton Cancer Support Group
	c/o 129 Conway Road, Hounslow, Middx TW4 5LP tel: 081-572 4821
Aims	To provide a cancer support group
Partners	Volunteers trained by organisations such as BACUP, Cancerlink and New Approaches to Cancer/local GPs/primary care team

Project Number 23	Sunderland Laryngectomy Club c/o 7 Buttermere Avenue, Easington Lane, Hetton le Hole, Tyne and Wear DH5 0PP tel: 091-526 9780
Aims	To provide a support group for people who have had laryngectomies
Partners	Local health education centre/Sunderland Laryngectomy Club
Project Number 24	Health Education for Women Training Project c/o Women's Health Unit, Field Development Division, Health Education Authority, Hamilton House, Mabledon Place, London WC1H 9TX tel: 071-383 3833
Aims	To provide training for women's health education
Partners	Health Education Authority/Workers' Educational Association
Project Number 25	Girls and Young Women's Health Project c/o Varley Street Clinic, Farnborough Road, Miles Platting, Manchester M10 8EE tel: 061-205 6111
Aims	To provide a service on women's health developed and controlled by young women themselves
Partners	Manchester Council for Voluntary Services/District Health Authority/Manchester City Council/local education department
Project Number 26	Worcester Cancer Support Group c/o 31 Calgary Drive, Lower Wick, Worcester WR2 4DW tel: 0905 422654
Aims	To collaborate in providing community care to cancer patients
Partners	Local hospital/local nursing manager/local specialist nursing teams/Worcester Cancer Support Group
Project Number 27	Leicester City Council Environmental Health Office, Leicester City Council, New Walk Centre, Welford Place, Leicester LE1 6ZG tel: 0533 549922
Aims	To help and support voluntary groups as part of the remit of the Environmental Health Office
Partners	Environmental Health Office/local voluntary organisations
Project Number 28	Cancercare Cancercare, Slynedales, Lancaster Road, Slyne, Lancaster LA2 6AW tel: 0524 381820
Aims	To provide a holistic approach to the care of cancer patients
Partners	St John's Hospice/Cancercare/Royal Lancaster Infirmary/District Health Authority
Project Number 29	National Community Health Resource Training Project c/o National Community Health Resource, 57 Chalton Street, London NW1 tel: 071-383 3841
Aims	To provide training to a mixture of voluntary/statutory staff
Partners	NCHR/Health Education Authority
Project Number 30	East Birmingham Health Authority, Health Promotion Unit c/o Health Education Department, East Birmingham Health Authority, 102 Blakesley Road, Yardley, Birmingham B25 8RN tel: 021-783 3358
Aims	To develop community links and develop concrete programmes, for example to encourage black and ethnic minority communities to address HIV and AIDS issues
Partners	Birmingham Health Authority/various voluntary bodies locally

Project Number 31 Regional Working Party in Black and Ethnic Minorities Employment Group
c/o Blackburn and District Community Relations Council, 11 Richmond Terrace, Blackburn BB1 7BD tel: 0254 61924
Aims Summary of annual review responses to District Health Authorities including equal opportunities policies, service delivery, draft strategy for future work
Partners Four of the North West's Community Relations Councils/Council for Voluntary Services

Project Number 32 Blackburn, Hyndburn and Ribble Valley Health Authority Ethnic Minorities Steering Group
Blackburn and District Community Relations Council
Aims To provide consultation and feedback on minority ethnic issues and to review all aspects of health authority provision for ethnic minorities
Partners Blackburn CRC/Community Health Council/FHSA/District Health Authority/local authority/Health Promotion Unit

Project Number 33 Corby Asian Association Health Fair
Wellingborough Racial Equality Council, c/o Victoria Centre, Park Road, Wellingborough NN8 1HT tel: 0933 278000
Aims To run a health fair focusing on Asian issues
Partners Corby Asian Association/Kettering Health Authority/Social Services

Project Number 34 Hertfordshire Hearing Advisory Service
Hertfordshire Deafness Support Association, The Woodside Centre, The Commons, Welwyn Garden City, Herts AL7 4SE tel: 0707 324582
Aims To provide a county-wide visiting service for elderly and hard of hearing people
Volunteers visit to carry out simple maintenance and paid advice
Partners Volunteers/Social Services/Herts County Council/Hertfordshire Health Authority

Project Number 35 National No Smoking Day
Smoking Education Programme, Health Education Authority, Hamilton House, Mabledon Place, London WC1H 9TX tel: 071-383 3833
Aims Co-ordinated activities to help people reduce/stop smoking
Partners Action Against Smoking and Health (ASH)/Parents Against Tobacco (PAT)/HEA

Project Number 36 Health First
Bates Green Health Centre, Bates Green, Norwich NR5 8YT tel: 0603 749921
Aims To provide health promotion and support, based at a GP surgery, for low-income families
Partners Local GP/voluntary workers

Project Number 37 Abbeyfield Affiliated Scheme for Elderly Ex-psychiatric Patients
c/o Jewish Care, 221 Golders Green Road, London NW11 9DQ tel: 081-458 3282 x350
Aims To bring out five elderly ex-psychiatric patients back to their original community
Partners Jewish Care/Enfield Health Authority

Project Number 38 Hull Healthy Cities
c/o Central Policy Unit, Hull City Council, The Guildhall, Alfred Gelder Street, Hull HU1 2AA tel: 0482 595024
Aims Part of Healthy Cities Network – aims to make Hull a healthier city for all its residents by encouraging community participation in health issues
Partners Local authority/health authority/voluntary sector

Project Number 39	Sefton Women's Advisory Network Drop-in Centre (SWAN) c/o Health Promotion Unit, Fazakerley Hospital, Liverpool L9 7AL tel: 051-529 3325
Aims	To set up a women's health group
Partners	SWAN/Health Promotion Unit, South Sefton Health Authority

Project Number 40	Women's Health Information Centre/Pregnancy Testing Service c/o 68 Chesswood Road, Worthing, Sussex BN11 2AG tel: 0903 202925
Aims	To set up a women's health information centre
Partners	Women's Health Information Centre/Worthing District Health Authority

Project Number 41	Health Matters for All Midlands Radio Action Trust, c/o Mercia FM, Hertford Place, Coventry CV1 3TT tel: 0203 633933
Aims	To devise a range of Asian health programmes to be broadcast in the Leicester and Coventry areas
Partners	Midlands Radio Action Trust/Department of Health

Project Number 42	UK Health for All Network c/o PO Box 101, Liverpool, L69 5BE tel: 051-231 1009
Aims	To promote the UK Healthy Cities Network
Partners	Health authority/local authority/voluntary sector

Project Number 43	Age Well Initiatives c/o Age Concern England, 1268 London Road, London SW16 4EJ tel: 081-679 8000
Aims	To provide a multidisciplinary way of working in support of good health for older people. A database of local projects exists
Partners	Various health authorities/health promotion units around the country/Centre for Health and Retirement Education

Project Number 44	Fire Safety Mobile Unit c/o Age Concern England, 1268 London Road, London SW16 4EJ tel: 081-679 8000
Aims	To provide a mobile advice service and inform older people about fire safety in the home
Partners	Home Office/ACE/fire brigade/private sector heating companies

Project Number 45	Keep Warm, Keep Well c/o Age Concern England, 1268 London Road, London SW16 4EJ tel: 081-679 8000
Aims	To provide a helpline dealing with heating problems – primarily, though not exclusively, for the elderly
Partners	ACE/Help the Aged/Neighbourhood Energy Action

Project Number 46	The New Dimensions Centre for Holistic Life 33 Eriswell Road, Worthing, West Sussex BN11 3HP tel: 0903 203598
Aims	To organise quarterly seminars for orthodox and complementary medicine
Partners	New Dimensions Centre (self-funding)/local GPs

Project Number 47	Newham Alcohol Advisory Service (NAAS) 7 Sebert Road, Newham, London E7 0NG tel: 081-519 3354
Aims	To provide an alcohol advisory service locally
Partners	Local authority/Health Promotion Unit/voluntary organisation

Project Number 48	Great Yarmouth and Waveney Health Promotion Venture
	Northgate Hospital, Northgate Street, Great Yarmouth, Norfolk NR30 1BU
	tel: 0493 856222
Aims	The philosophy of the Health Promotion Unit is to work with voluntary groups
Partners	Health Promotion Unit/local voluntary groups

Project Number 49	Albany Health Project Market Stall
	c/o Albany Centre, Douglas Way, Deptford, London SE8 4AG tel: 081-692 0231
Aims	To provide a stall each week in Deptford market dealing with a variety of health issues
Partners	Albany Health Project/Waldron Health Centre (health visitors)

Project Number 50	The Breakthrough Trust Deaf–Hearing Integration
	Birmingham Centre, Selly Oak Colleges, Bristol Road, Birmingham B29 6LE
	tel: 021-472 6447
Aims	To produce a guide to local services for hearing-impaired people
Partners	Five Birmingham District Health Authorities/Breakthrough Trust

Project Number 51	Wellington Health Education Resource Enterprise (WHERE)
	The Portakabin, Fore Street Car Park, Wellington, Somerset tel: 0823 665896
Aims	To provide an information resource on health matters
Partners	WHERE/GPs/health visitors/Taunton Deane Borough Council/Somerset Health Authority

Project Number 52	Cambridge Community Development Health Project
	c/o The Shed, Addenbrooke's, Hills Road, Cambridge CB2 2QQ tel: 0223 26686
Aims	To set up a community health project
Partners	Community groups in King's Hedges, East Barnwall Districts/Cambridge District Health Authority Health Promotion Unit

Project Number 53	Choice! For the Right to Choose a Healthy Vegetarian Meal at School
	c/o The Vegetarian Society UK Ltd, Parkdale, Dunham Road, Altrincham, Cheshire WA14 4DQ tel: 061-928 0793
Aims	To promote healthy balanced vegetarian meals in schools via four-week menu planners and nutritional guidelines for schools
Partners	Local authority catering managers/The Vegetarian Society UK Ltd

Project Number 54	St Erme House Autistic Community
	St Erme, Truro, Cornwall TR4 9BW tel: 0841 520969
Aims	To provide a specialist unit for people suffering from autism, including day-centre training
Partners	Devon and Cornwall Autistic Society/Cornwall and Isles of Scilly Health Authority/Devon Health Authority

Project Number 55	Leicester Community Health Project
	c/o Voluntary Action Leicester, 32 De Montfort Street, Leicester LE1 7GD
	tel: 0533 555600
Aims	A community health initiative including drop-in, health centre user group, pregnancy-testing network, shared teaching and trainers
Partners	Voluntary Action Leicester/Leicester Health Authority

Project Number 56	Family Welfare Association, Lewisham Shared Housing Scheme
	Family Welfare Association 219 Stanstead Road, London SE23 1HU tel: 081-690 4422
Aims	To provide housing for long-term mentally ill people
Partners	Family Welfare Association/Lewisham and North Southwark District Health Authority/Shackleton and Hyde Housing Association
Project Number 57	Stockwell Health Project
	c/o 460 Wandsworth Road, London SW8 3LX tel: 071-622 9455
Aims	To develop a number of community projects
Partners	Lady Margaret Hall Settlement/West Lambeth Health Authority
Project Number 58	Cancer Winners
	Omega House, New Street, Margate, Kent CT9 1EG tel: 0843 297360
Aims	To provide a self-help cancer support group
Partners	Voluntary organisation/local medical and nursing provision
Project Number 59	Dialabetic
	The British Diabetic Association, c/o 10 Queen Anne Street, London W1M 0BD tel: 071-323 1531
Aims	To provide a telephone counselling service for people with diabetes
Partners	Northampton Branch of BDA/Northampton General Hospital
Project Number 60	Age Well Initiative – A Healthy Living Adviser
	c/o District Health Promotion Manager, Education Centre, Avenue House, The Avenue, Eastbourne, East Sussex BN21 3XY tel: 0323 37121
Aims	To focus activities of twelve Age Concern groups currently active within the Eastbourne Health Authority area and to support further groups
Partners	Age Concern East Sussex/Eastbourne Health Authority
Project Number 61	Nottingham Council for Voluntary Service (various partnerships)
	33 Mansfield Road, Nottingham NG1 3FF tel: 0602 476714
Aims	To work in partnership, in a number of ways, including: students on social work to work under supervision on Community Health Care Projects for the health authority; publication of *Nottingham Help Directory* – bringing together NCVS, library services and health authority to publish an annual directory of helping agencies within the Health Authority area; community radio team, who provide air-time to community health projects
Partners	NCVS/Nottingham Health Authority/Social Services
Project Number 62	Whiteway Health Project
	36 St Michaels Road, Whiteway, Bath BA2 1PZ tel: 0225 331243
Aims	To provide a number of community health initiatives – including playscheme and women's network
Partners	Whiteway Health Project/clinical psychologists/local authority housing department
Project Number 63	Health Matters
	47A Fleet Street, Swindon SN1 1RE tel: 0793 618558
Aims	To work with and support people who are carers or involved in self-help support groups
Partners	Health Matters/Swindon Health Authority/Wiltshire County Council/Allied Dunbar

Project Number 64	Emmanuel Church Drop-in Centre
	c/o Voluntary Services Organiser, Bolton General Hospital, Minerva Road, Farnworth, Bolton BL4 0JR tel: 0204 390720
Aims	To provide a preventive mental health project. The church provides a social and recreational facility for people 'experiencing life problems and undue stress'. The group 'enables people to meet with professionals in a relaxed atmosphere'.
Partners	Emmanuel Church/Bolton Health Authority/Bolton Social Services

Project Number 65	Coventry Women's Health and Information Centre
	Coventry and Warwickshire Hospital Site, Stoney Stanton Road, Coventry CV1 4FH tel: 0203 714082
Aims	To bring together the voluntary and statutory sectors to provide a comprehensive service for women in Coventry
Partners	Coventry Women's Health Network/Coventry Health Authority

Project Number 66	Southwark Phoenix Women's Health Organisation
	140 Friern Road, East Dulwich, London SE22 0AY tel: 081-693 8956
Aims	To provide a community based women's health project. Its goal is 'to help women, particularly those from ethnic minorities, to help themselves to better health and general well-being'
Partners	Southwark Women's Health Organisation/Department of Health through consortium of Opportunities for Volunteering

Project Number 67	Sobell House Bereavement Service
	c/o Sir Michael Sobell House, Churchill Hospital, Oxford OX3 7LJ tel: 0865 751156
Aims	To provide a bereavement counselling service for relatives of those who have died from cancer. They have published a number of booklets and offer training information and support to a wide range of people (for example, GP trainees, medical students, nursing staff, theological students and community groups) from all areas
Partners	NHS/hospice volunteers from Sir Michael Sobell House

Project Number 68	Dallam Health Project
	c/o Warrington Community Project, Staff House 2, Vulcan Close, Padgate, Warrington, Cheshire WA2 0HL
Aims	To provide a community based health project flowing from the philosophy of 'Health for All'
Partners	The Children's Society/borough council/Health Authority/Department of Community Medicine and Health Promotion

Project Number 69	Waterloo Health Project
	c/o 5 Munro House, Murphy Street, London SE1 7AJ tel: 071-633 0852
Aims	To provide a number of health project services in the Waterloo area of South-east London
Partners	West Lambeth Health Authority/local health visitor/Waterloo Health Project

Project Number 70	Tower Hamlets Health Strategy Group
	Oxford House, Derbyshire Street, London E2 6HG tel: 071-256 0163
Aims	To provide a health promotion service for Asian clients, including health promotion sessions in mosques, support for health bus, bilingual pest control officers
Partners	THHSG/Neighbourhood Energy Action/Community Job Link/London East Mosque/Tenants' Federation/Tower Hamlets Health Authority/local EHOs

Project Number 71	Home Visiting Link Scheme
	St Swithins Institute, The Trinity, Worcester WR1 2PN tel: 0905 25121
Aims	To visit ethnic minority families and provide other advice/assistance on health issues
Partners	Department of Health (project funded through Opportunities for Volunteering/ Worcester Racial Equality Council)
Project Number 72	Oxford City Council Health Promotion Unit
	Health Promotion Team, Environmental Health Department, Thomas Hull House, 1 Bonn Square, Oxford OX1 1QH tel: 0865 249811
Aims	To work with the community
Partners	Environmental Health Department/numerous voluntary/ community organisations
Project Number 73	Mental Health Education
	Mental Health Tutor/Organiser, 4 Whitby Avenue, Stackton Lane, York YO3 0ET tel: 0904 424653
Aims	To provide an adult education programme for people with mental health problems
Partners	Workers' Educational Association/York Health Authority
Project Number 74	School Meals Evaluation Project
	Forum for Coronary Heart Disease Prevention, Hamilton House, Mabledon Place, London WC1H 9TX tel: 071-282 3933
Aims	To produce a school meals evaluation package to run on computers
Partners	Health Education Authority/various voluntary organisations/Hampstead Health Promotion Unit/dietitians/schools
Project Number 75	New Speakers Club
	c/o Manchester Royal Infirmary, Oxford Road, Manchester M13 9WL tel: 061-276 4131
Aims	To provide a support club for laryngectomees in the Manchester area (includes information and social events)
Partners	Manchester Health Authority (speech therapists)/laryngectomees
Project Number 76	Health Education for Women Training Project
	Workers' Educational Association, North Western District, 4th Floor, Crawford House, Precinct Centre, Oxford Road, Manchester M13 9GH tel: 061-273 7652
Aims	To produce a women's health training manual
Partners	Workers' Educational Association (three districts)/Health Education Authority
Project Number 77	The Horticultural Therapy Centre for Horticulture and the Environment
	Trunkwell View, Beech Hill, near Reading, Berks RG7 2AS tel: 0734 883130
Aims	To promote understanding of the value of horticulture and the natural environment in health and welfare of disabled people
Partners	Society for Horticultural Therapy/Bulmershe Centre (Reading)/Reading Social Services
Project Number 78	Amnass Homes Project
	Amnass, St Charles Hospital, Exmoor Street, London W10 6DZ tel: 081-969 0796
Aims	To plan long-term care facilities for brain-injured people
Partners	Amnesia Association/Paddington Churches' Housing Association/Parkside District Health Authority

Project Number 79	Health Teaching with Small Community Groups
	Birchills Community Centre, Farringdon Street, Walsall WS2 8UH tel: 0922 721207
Aims	To teach health awareness in the community
Partners	Birchills CE Schools Community Association/Walsall Health Authority
Project Number 80	Leicestershire Laryngectomee Club
	12 Hockley Farm Road, Leicester LE3 1HG tel: 0533 858592
Aims	To provide support for local laryngectomees and their families
Partners	Leicestershire Health Authority Speech Therapy Department/laryngectomees
Project Number 81	Blakelaw Young Parents Support Group
	c/o Newcastle CVS, MEA House, Ellison Place, Newcastle upon Tyne NE1 8XS tel: 091-232 7445
Aims	To provide a co-ordinated approach to support pregnant women, young parents and their children whose needs are not adequately met by traditional statutory services
Partners	Newcastle CVS/community midwives/health visitors
Project Number 82	Tower Hamlets Health Project
	Oxford House, Derbyshire Street, London E2 6HG tel: 071-739 9001
Aims	To provide a drop-in service for women with special mental health needs
Partners	Oxford House/Tower Hamlets Health Authority
Project Number 83	Meningitis Trust
	Meningitis Trust, Fern House, Bath Road, Stroud, Glos GL3 3TJ tel: 0453 751738
Aims	To increase awareness of meningitis and to support sufferers and their families
Partners	Meningitis Trust/Department of Health/Gloucester Health Authority/other health authorities throughout England and Wales
Project Number 84	Addenbrooke's Hospital, Cambridge – Radioactivity Naturally Occurring in Young Girls
	c/o Addenbrooke's Hospital, Cambridge CB2 2QQ tel: 0223 245151
Aims	Part of programme to develop health awareness – measurement of base level radioactivity as occurring naturally in human beings
Partners	Cambridge East Girl Guides/Cambridge Health Authority
Project Number 85	Smokers' Quitline and National Smoking Cessation Resource Centre
	102 Gloucester Place, London W1H 3DA; tel: 071-487 2858
Aims	To establish a helpline for smokers and found a resource centre for smoking cessation (Quitline number 071-487 3000)
Partners	Quit/Health Education Authority
Project Number 86	493 Project
	Association for Prevention of Addiction, 5–7 Tavistock Place, London WC1H 9SS tel: 071-383 5071
Aims	To provide a service – primarily harm minimisation/reduction for people with injecting drug use
Partners	APA/Tower Hamlets Regional Health Authority, City and Hackney Health Authority

Project Number 87	AIDS Ahead
	144 London Road, Northwich, Cheshire tel: 0606 47047 (voice) and 0606 330472 (text)
Aims	To provide AIDS/HIV services and support within the deaf community
Partners	British Deaf Association/Department of Health/Health Education Authority/ various Regional Health Authorities/District Health Authorities

Project Number 88	Hospice at Home
	The Care Foundation, Michael Tetley Hall, Sandhurst Road, Tunbridge Wells, Kent TN2 3JS tel: 0892 544877
Aims	To provide a team of nursing sisters and volunteers who take the skills and care of the hospice movement into people's homes
Partners	Hospice at Home/Tunbridge Wells Health Authority

Project Number 89	Al-Anon
	61 Great Dover Street, London SE1 4YF tel: 071-403 0888
Aims	Help for family and close friends of problem drinkers
	No longer involved in partnership

Project Number 90	Parkside Health Promotion Unit
	Parkside Health Promotion Unit, Green Lodge, Barretts Green Road, London NW10 7AP tel: 081-965 6566
Aims	To work with voluntary organisations
Partners	Health Promotion Unit/various local groups

Project Number 91	Broadcasting Support Service Helplines
	252 Western Avenue, London W3 6XJ tel: 081-992 5522
Aims	To mount helplines for broadcasters (particularly National AIDS Helpline); dial-and-listen services
Partners	Department of Health/other government ministries/BSS (charity)

Project Number 92	Lewisham Alcohol Advisory Council
	Wendy Block, 21 Slagrove Place, London SE13 7XW tel: 081-690 0203
Aims	To increase public awareness of alcohol problems. Also runs initiatives such as Alcohol and Young People Project
Partners	Lewisham and North Southwark Alcohol Advisory Council/Lewisham and North Southwark Health Authority/Metropolitan Police

Project Number 93	Haemophilia, AIDS and Safer Sex: The Choice is Here
	c/o The Haemophilia Society, 123 Westminster Bridge Road, London SE1 7HR tel: 071-928 2020
Aims	To produce a well-designed and positive guide to safer sex for haemophiliacs
Partners	The Haemophilia Society/Health Education Authority

Project Number 94	Sevenoaks Information Centre (at Sevenoaks Hospital)
	c/o Sevenoaks District Volunteer Bureau, 34 Buckhurst Avenue, Sevenoaks, Kent TN13 1LZ tel: 0732 454785
Aims	To provide volunteers for the information desk and volunteers to sit with seriously and terminally ill patients
Partners	Sevenoaks Volunteer Bureau/The Care Foundation (Hospice at Home – see No. 88)

Project Number 95	Women's Health and Diet Group
	c/o Rushcliffe CVS, Civic Centre, Pavilion Road, West Bridgford, Nottingham NG2 5FE tel: 0602 816988
Aims	To provide advice on women's health for women at work during the day (and therefore not able to take advantage of normal adult education classes)
Partners	Nottingham Health Authority/Health Promotion Unit/Rushcliffe CVS
Project Number 96	North Tyneside Council Women's Unit
	Women's Officer, Town Hall, High Street, Wallsend NE28 7RR tel: 091-262 7371
Aims	To provide support for issues related to women in the North Tyneside area
Partners	North Tyneside County Council/various community groups
Project Number 97	The Generalist Advisers AIDS Training Project
	c/o AIDS Project, FIAC, 13 Stockwell Road, London SW9 9AU tel: 071-274 1839
Aims	To promote good practice in the management of AIDS advice projects
Partners	Federation of Independent Advice Centres/Greater London CABx/Health Education Authority/National AIDS Trust
Project Number 98	Sunderland Health Information Centre
	223 High Street West, Sunderland SR1 1TZ tel: 091-510 0249
Aims	To support self-help groups and provide health-related information to the public
Partners	Sunderland Health Authority/self-help groups
Project Number 99	Preston Health Promotion Unit/Red Rose Radio
	Preston Health Promotion Unit, Preston Health Authority, Watling Street Road, Fulwood, Preston, Lancs PR2 4DX tel: 0772 711215
Aims	To disseminate information on health issues using local radio
Partners	Red Rose Radio/Preston Health Promotion Unit
Project Number 100	North-east CAB Multi-agency Resource Centre
	NACABx North-east Area, 19 Enterprise House, Kingsway North, Team Valley Trading Estate, Gateshead, Tyne and Wear NE11 0SR tel: 091-482 5522
Aims	To provide a multi-agency resource facility
Partners	South Tees Health Authority/CABx
Project Number 101	Centre for Policy on Ageing
	Information pack on services in the area covered by Cripplegate Foundation
	Centre for Policy on Ageing, 25–31 Ironmonger Row, London EC1V 3QP tel: 071-253 1787
Aims	To produce 1000 copies of information pack, hold training sessions on how to use it, monitor and assess effectiveness of work
Partners	CPA/wide variety of statutory and non-statutory bodies
Project Number 102	Northdale Horticultural Project
	12 Friarage Street, Northallerton, North Yorkshire DL6 1DP tel: 0609 70269
Aims	To provide opportunities for horticultural training and employment for people with a mental handicap
Partners	Northallerton and Dales Mencap/Northallerton and District CHC

Project Number 103	Living Options
	Secretary, Northallerton and District CHC, 66 High Street, Northallerton, North Yorkshire DL7 8ER tel: 0609 770627
Aims	Part of national Living Options Programme to define goals for service provision for people with severe physical and sensory disabilities. Aims to set up and monitor systems that deliver the elements of a comprehensive service for people with disabilities
Partners	King's Fund/Northallerton and District CHC/local disabled organisations/community groups
Project Number 104	Eastwood Tuesday Club
	c/o Eastwood Volunteer Bureau, 89A Nottingham Road, Eastwood, Nottingham NG16 3AJ tel: 0773 710238
Aims	To provide 'an enjoyable time out for senile dementia sufferers and a break for their carers in what is a rural area'
Partners	Eastwood Volunteer Bureau/Nottingham Health Authority
Project Number 105	Sittingbourne/Sheppey Connections
	c/o Swale Volunteer Bureau, Central House, Central Avenue, Sittingbourne, Kent ME10 4NT tel: 0795 473828
Aims	To provide additional support to people who are experiencing a mental health problem and need help to regain their confidence – including a one-to-one befriending scheme and drop-in facility
Partners	Swale Volunteer Bureau/Mental Health Team, Kent County Council Social Services
Project Number 106	Pennywell Neighbourhood Centre
	128 Plawsworth Square, Pennywell, Sunderland, Tyne and Wear SR4 9DE tel: 091-534 1477
Aims	To set up a neighbourhood house from which a variety of health workers and others undertake group work and initiatives
Partners	Save the Children Fund/Sunderland Health Authority/Sunderland Borough Council
Project Number 107	Cowgate Children's Centre
	Meadowdale Crescent, Cowgate Estate, Newcastle upon Tyne NE5 3HL tel: 091-286 5507
Aims	To provide a playgroup for 40 children with activities for parents on healthy eating and lifestyles
Partners	Save the Children Fund/Newcastle Social Services Department/Newcastle Health Authority/local residents
Project Number 108	Riverside Child Health Project
	The Clinic, Atkinson Road, Benwell, Newcastle upon Tyne NE4 8XS tel: 091-272 2949/091-273 9730
Aims	To provide a group work programme and outreach work, including the design and distribution of material for minority groups
Partners	Save the Children Fund/Newcastle Health Authority/Newcastle City Council/Inner City Partnership (Department of the Environment)

Project Number 109	The Parkin Project: Going for Growth Project Co-ordinator, Save the Children Fund, North East Sub Office, F Floor, Milburn House, Dean Street, Newcastle NE1 1LF tel: 091 230 0694
Aims	An initiative to develop a community-based primary preventive response to low growth rates among inner city children
Partners	Newcastle Health Authority/Save the Children Fund/NSPCC/Newcastle University Department of Child Health

Project Number 110	West Yorkshire Travellers Project c/o Save the Children Fund, 2nd Floor, National Deposit House, 1 Eastgate, Leeds LS2 7LY tel: 0532 42482
Aims	To provide better access to services – particularly health – for the Traveller community
Partners	Save the Children Fund/Leeds East and West Health Authorities

Project Number 111	Health Support for Vietnamese and West African Women, Children and their Families Deptford Family Resource Centre, 1A Daubeny Tower, Bowditch, Pepys Estate, Deptford, London SE8 3QW tel: 081-743 3311
Aims	To provide wider understanding of the child in the context of his/her family and culture, to identify specific needs and to encourage a multi-disciplinary approach to family needs
Partners	Save the Children Fund/Deptford Family Resource Centre/The Newcomen Centres (Guy's Hospital)/North Southwark and Lewisham Health Authority

Project Number 112	Good Mental Health Project TACT Project, East Community Centre, Moor Terrace, Hendon, Sunderland tel: 0783 77051
Aims	To develop a 'vision' where economic, social and environmental factors allow people to feel in control of their own lives as part of a caring community
Partners	Neighbourhood network/health authority workers from Mental Health Service, Social Services and Housing

Project Number 113	Lewisham and North Southwark Health Promotion Unit South Wing Nurses' Home, Lewisham Hospital, High Street, London SE13 6LH tel: 081-690 4311
Aims	To develop partnerships with the community
Partners	Health Promotion Unit/community groups

Project Number 114	East Birmingham Day Centre 66 Wordsworth Road, Small Heath, Birmingham B70 8EZ tel: 021-500 5988
Aims	To develop various projects including provision of employment project (Footprint); development of a housing consortium; drop-in club; 7-day a week service
Partners	National Schizophrenia Fellowship/East Birmingham Health Authority/user group for the area (LIBRA)

Project Number 115	Manchester Self-help Resource Centre PO Box 309, Manchester M60 2FG tel: 061-226 5225
Aims	To work with self-help groups
Partners	Health authority/local authority/voluntary organisation

Project Number 116	Calderdale Health Education
	Health Education Centre, 47 Crown Street, Halifax, West Yorkshire HX1 1JB tel: 0422 366733
Aims	The Health Education Unit facilitates and supports initiatives that promote self-help, raise confidence, increase skills and information
Partners	Health Education Unit/community groups
Project Number 117	Learning about AIDS pack
	Department of Education, Bristol Polytechnic, Redland Hill, Bristol BS6 6UZ tel: 0272 656261
Aims	Development of resource material for those working in the field of AIDS
Partners	Bristol Polytechnic/Health Education Authority/voluntary organisations
Project Number 118	Richmond Fellowship Community Mental Health Project
	The Richmond Fellowship, 8 Addison Road, Kensington, London W14 8DL tel: 071-603 6373
Aims	To set up residential communities for ex long-stay mental hospital patients
Partners	Richmond Fellowship/MIND/Various health authorities
Project Number 119	Healthy Sheffield 2000
	c/o Town Hall Chambers, 1 Barkers Pool, Sheffield S1 1EN tel: 0742 734645/ 735390
Aims	Part of the UK Healthy Cities Network; many community-based health initiatives
Partners	Sheffield City Council, Community Health Council, Commission for Racial Equality/Sheffield District Health Authority/Voluntary Action Sheffield
Project Number 120	Brent Sickle Cell and Thalassaemia Centre
	Brent Sickle Cell and Thalassaemia Centre, Central Middlesex Hospital, London NW10 7NS tel: 081-453 2262/2685
Aims	To provide counselling to sickle cell sufferers
Partners	Central Middlesex Hospital/volunteers from family support groups
Project Number 121	Youth Outreach, Colchester
	c/o Health Promotion Unit, Essex County Hospital, Lexden Road, Colchester, Essex CO3 3NB tel: 0206 853535
Aims	To provide an outreach service to help young people on sensitive issues
Partners	Health Promotion Unit/Youth Enquiry Service
Project Number 122	Coming out in Colchester
	c/o Health Promotion Unit, Essex County Hospital, Lexden Road, Colchester, Essex CO3 3NB tel: 0206 853535
Aims	To make it safe for gay men to come out in Colchester
Partners	Colchester Area Gay Community/Health Promotion Unit
Project Number 123	East Dorset Health Promotion Unit
	St Leonards Hospital, Nr Ringwood, Hampshire BH24 2RR tel: 0202 871165
Aims	To promote joint activities between the public and the voluntary sector in the areas of older people and women's health
Partners	Age Concern/Well Women Centre/Health Promotion Unit
Project Number 124	Staff HIV Training
	Health Promotion Unit, Essex County Hospital, Lexden Road, Colchester, Essex CO3 3NB tel: 0206 853535
Aims	To train CABx staff in issues which surround HIV
Partners	Health Promotion Unit/people with HIV-related problems

Project Number 125	Chelmsford and Colchester Breast Screening Service with Colchester Hospital League of Friends c/o Health Promotion Unit, Essex County Hospital, Lexden Road, Colchester, Essex CO3 3NB tel: 0206 853535
Aims	To promote breast screening along with fund-raising activities on behalf of the service
Partners	Colchester Hospital League of Friends/Chelmsford and Colchester Breast Screening Service

Project Number 126	Neuro-Care Team Motor Neurone Disease Association (MNDA), PO Box 246, Northampton NN1 2PR tel: 0604 250505
Aims	To provide an enhanced standard of care to people diagnosed with any of the conditions below at Harold Wood Hospital, Romford. Patient-centred approach with patients/carers involved in the management of their conditions
Partners	Parkinson's Disease Society/Multiple Sclerosis Society (local), MNDA, Friedrich's Ataxia, Dystonia/Barking, Havering, Brentwood District Health Authority

Project Number 127	Cancer care leaflet c/o Council for Voluntary Service for Harrogate and Area, 6 Victoria Avenue, Harrogate HG1 1ED tel: 0423 504074
Aims	To produce and distribute a leaflet on cancer
Partners	Voluntary organisations (18)/Social Services/CHC/Cancer Relief/Macmillan Fund

Project Number 128	CLASH (Central London Action on Street Health) 15 Bateman Buildings, Soho Square, London W1V 5TW tel: 071-437 0752
Aims	To provide information, support and outreach
Partners	CLASH/Bloomsbury Health Authority/Health Education Department/Hungerford Drug Project/Terrence Higgins Trust/Basement Youth Project

Project Number 129	The Health Store c/o Health Promotion Service, Riversley Park Clinic, Coton Road, Nuneaton, Warwickshire CV11 5TY tel: 0203 340035
Aims	Provide a confidential counselling/health promotion service to young people
Partners	Talking Shop/North Warwickshire Health Promotion Service/Social Services/Youth Service

Project Number 130	Family Planning Association 25–35 Mortimer Street, London W1N 7RJ tel: 071-636 7866
Aims	To provide information and advice on family planning and contraception – the Family Planning Promotion Service
Partners	FPA/Department of Health/Health Education Authority

Project Number 131	North Tees Health Promotion Service North Tees Hospital, Hardwick, Stockton on Tees, Cleveland TS19 0EA tel: 0642 677701
Aims	To provide liaison, advice, and help with selection of suitable volunteers; projects are run in the area of women's health, alcohol, drugs and HIV/AIDS
Partners	North Tees Health Promotion Unit/North Tees District Health Authority/North Tees Volunteers

Project Number 132	Wandsworth Volunteer Bureau – Development Worker, Mental Health
	Wandsworth Volunteer Bureau, 170 Garrett Lane, London SW18 4DA tel: 081-870 4319
Aims	To recognise the value of people who have experienced drug and alcohol problems and of using these people to help others as a resource for 'care in the community'
Partners	Wandsworth Volunteer Bureau/Wandsworth Borough Council/Wandsworth Health Authority

Project Number 133	Ask – Lincoln Youth Counselling and Information Service
	Ask, 11a St Mary's Street, Lincoln LN5 7EQ tel: 0522 513564
Aims	To provide a confidential youth counselling service
Partners	Ask (a Lincoln CVS project)/North Lincolnshire Health Authority

Project Number 134	Outset
	Information Officer, Outset, Drake House, 18 Creekside, London SE8 3DZ tel: 081-692 7141
Aims	To develop training for people with mental health problems
Partners	South Bedfordshire Health Authority/Outset

Project Number 135	Oxford Project for Prevention of Heart Attack and Stroke
	Project Director, The Oxford Project, c/o The HEA Primary Care Unit, Block 10, Churchill Hospital, Oxford OX3 7LJ tel: 0865 63283
Aims	To provide free health checks in general practices
Partners	The Chest, Heart and Stroke Association/Oxfordshire Health Authority/Department of Health/Health Education Authority

Project Number 136	Bolsover Mental Health Roadshow
	North Derbyshire Health Promotion Service, Scarsdale Hospital, Newbold Road, Chesterfield, Derbyshire tel: 0246 231255 x 277
Aims	To work in partnership with the community – for example, in organising a roadshow to promote positive mental health
Partners	Health Promotion Unit/various local groups

Project Number 137	Health for All 2000
	Southend Action Group for the Homeless
	Southend Association of Voluntary Services, 484 Southchurch Road, Southend, Essex SS1 2QA tel: 0702 619489
Aims	To provide a shelter for homeless people
Partners	SAVS/Children's Society/Southend Centre for the Homeless/Southend Council of Churches/Southend Health Authority/Social Services

Project Number 138	Hyperactive Children's Support Group
	71 Whyke Lane, Chichester, West Sussex PO19 2LD tel: 0243 551313/0903 725182
Aims	To work in partnership with health visitors to identify causes of hyperactivity in children
Partners	Hyperactive Children's Support Group/health visitors

Project Number 139	Myatts Field Mobile Crèche
	5 Launderdale Houses, Cowley Estate, Gosling Way, London SW9 6JS tel: 071-735 7495
Aims	Health visitors refer new mothers to the mobile crèche and to the parent and baby group which holds discussions and shows videos on health issues
Partners	Mobile Crèche/health visitors at Myatts Field Health Centre

Project Number 140	Health Promotion Joint Planning Group
	Director of Public Health, Health Planners, Western Hospital/Michelle Goodman, Southampton Council of Community Service, 18 Oxford Street, Southampton, Hants SO1 1DJ tel: 0703 228291
Aims	To promote joint planning, including voluntary sector representatives who have contact with network of voluntary agencies
Partners	Health authority/Social Services/EHOs/Education Officers/Health for All co-ordinator/voluntary sector

Project Number 141	Arthritis Care – Hospital Information Points
	5 Grosvenor Crescent, London SW1X 7ER tel: 071-235 0902
Aims	To provide information points in hospital rheumatology clinics, staffed by members of Arthritis Care, explaining how the organisation can help people of all ages with arthritis
Partners	Arthritis Care/local hospitals

Appendix 7 USEFUL ADDRESSES AND OTHER INFORMATION

The Voluntary Agencies Directory is compiled annually by NCVO and published by Bedford Square Press. It lists over 2000 voluntary agencies in the UK. Available in person from NCVO or by post from Plymbridge Distributors, Estover Road, Plymouth PL6 7PZ. Price (1991): £10.95 plus £1.35 postage and packing.

ACRE (Action with Communities in Rural England), Stroud Road, Cirencester, Glos. GL7 6JR (tel: 0285 653477)

Age Concern England, Astral House, 1268 London Road, Norbury, London SW16 4EJ (tel: 081-679 8000)

Alcohol Concern, 305 Grays Inn Road, London WC1X 8QF (tel: 071-833 3471)

The Association of Community Health Councils for England and Wales (ASCHCE&W), 30 Drayton Park, London N5 1PB (tel: 081-609 8405)

Cancerlink, 17 Britannia Street, London WC1X 9JN (tel: 071-833 2451)

The Centre for Health and Retirement Education, Department of Educational Studies, Nodus Building, University of Surrey, Guildford GU2 5XH (tel: 0483 39390)

Charities Evaluation Services, Forbes House, 9 Artillery Lane, London E1 7LP (tel: 071-377 2939)

The Commission for Racial Equality, Elliott House, 10–12 Arlington Street, London SW1E 5EH (tel: 071-828 7022)

The Coronary Prevention Group, 102 Gloucester Place, London W1H 3DA (tel: 071-935 2889)

The Department of Health, Section 64, Grants Division, Wellington House, 133–155 Waterloo Road, London SE1 8UG (tel: 071-972 4108)

The Health Education Authority (Field Development Division), Hamilton House, Mabledon Place, London WC1H 9TX (tel: 071-383 3833)

The Health Education Authority Primary Health Care Unit, The Churchill Hospital, Old Road, Headington, Oxford OX3 7LJ (tel: 0865 226050)

The King's Fund Centre for Health Services Development, 126 Albert Street, London NW1 7NE (tel: 071-267 6111)

The Maternity Alliance, 15 Britannia Street, London WC1X 9JP (tel: 071-837 1265)

The National AIDS Trust, Room 1402, Euston Tower, 286 Euston Road, London NW1 3DN (tel: 071-388 1188 x3200)

The National Association of Health Authorities and Trusts, Chapter House, Chapter Street, London SW1P 4ND (tel: 071-233 7388)

National Community Health Resource (NCHR), 57 Chalton Street, London NW1 1HU (tel: 071-383 3841)

The National Council for Voluntary Organisations, 26 Bedford Square, London WC1B 3HU (tel: 071-636 4066)

The National Food Alliance, 102 Gloucester Place, London W1H 3DA (tel: 071-935 2889)

The National Self-help Support Centre, c/o NCVO, 26 Bedford Square, London WC1B 3HU

NCVO's Rural Unit, c/o NCVO, 26 Bedford Square, London WC1B 3HU

Patient Participation Groups: Hon. Sec., 50 Wallasey Village, Wallasey, Merseyside L45 3ML

The Primary Health Care Facilitator Scheme, c/o The Churchill Hospital, Old Road, Headington, Oxford OX3 7LJ

Project 26, 'The DHA Project', Department of Health, Room 914A, Richmond House, Whitehall, London SW1A 2NS (tel: 071-210 5259)

The Public Health Alliance, Room 204, Snow Hill House, 10–15 Livery Street, Birmingham B3 2PE (tel: 021-235 3698)

The Sickle Cell Society, Green Lodge, Barretts Green Road, London NW10 7AP (tel: 081-961 7795)

The Society of Health Education and Health Promotion Officers, c/o East Cumbria Health Authority, Health Education Unit, 11 Portland Square, Carlisle, Cumbria CA1 1PY (tel: 0228 515034)

UK Health for All Network, PO Box 101, Liverpool L69 5BE (tel: 051-231 1009)

The Volunteer Centre, 29 Lower Kings Road, Berkhamsted, Herts HP4 2AB (tel: 0442 873311)